LIFEWORKS

Behavioral Health in the Classroom

by
Nancy DiNatale, M.P.S., ATR
&
Hennie Shore

FOUNDATIONS
BEHAVIORAL HEALTH

LIFEWORKS

Published by Foundations Behavioral Health
833 E. Butler Avenue
Doylestown, PA 18901
215-345-0444

ISBN 0-9676106-0-5

Executive Publisher: Ronald T. Bernstein
Project Coordinator: Nancy DiNatale
Developmental Adviser: Beth Brody
Design and Illustration: Robert Burger

Acknowledgments

This book evolved from a Foundations Behavioral Health program currently offered to schools in need of behavioral health education for students, faculty, and parents. We created the LIFEWORKS program to offer a comprehensive school-based education component for at-risk children, dealing with emotional, behavioral, and family problems.

With the increasing prevalence of tragic school shootings throughout the country in the past year, school professionals are struggling to deal with the rise in violence that has plagued our educational institutions. *LIFEWORKS: Behavioral Health in the Classroom* offers teachers, counselors, school professionals, and families information on such violence, as well as a variety of other issues, including divorce, depression, substance abuse, aggression, family concerns, and other common problems.

This book would not have been possible without the contributions of the many individuals and colleagues who helped to make it a reality. We thank Ron Bernstein for his vision and unending support in guiding this book to publication, Catherine Barr for her guidance and direction, and Peggy Clay for keeping us on target at all times. A sincere thank you to our Editorial Advisory Committee members for contributing their valuable time and professional expertise. We also thank Beth Brody, Robert Burger, Diane Nussbaum, Rich Jensen, Laura Nash, Sheri Hartsoe, and Josh Strom for providing assistance when needed and help with all the many details that go into the creation of such a publication.

Editorial Advisory Committee

Introduction

Today's teachers have new responsibilities. In addition to looking after their students' educational progress, they find themselves looking after adolescents' emotional needs. Teachers must learn to be aware of red flags concerning emotional behavior and must be able to assess when "bad" behavior is simply a passing phase and when it is a symptom of a more severe underlying problem.

Students cannot learn to their full potential if they are struggling with the emotional baggage that they bring to school, and a successful education program must address students' emotional aspects as well as their cognitive abilities.

LIFEWORKS: Behavioral Health in the Classroom is designed to provide students with the information they need to understand, recognize, and cope with common problems such as anger, depression, substance abuse, and self-esteem.

Our purpose is not to give the particulars of a curriculum on specific subjects, but rather to provide basic but important information for use within the classroom. By integrating the easy-to-use activity sheets or the copy-ready material found in each chapter, *LIFEWORKS* can easily be woven into the daily curriculum. You can take what you need from each chapter and tailor the material to meet the needs of your students. Or, simply copy the sheets, hand them out, and begin the process of awareness and understanding.

The information in this guidebook deals with the real issues that are affecting our students today. Students want to talk about these issues, and this guidebook gives them the floor.

Some material is repeated—both from one chapter to another and even within a chapter. This is because problem-solving strategies often overlap, and because we wish to be successful in driving home important messages. Stating an idea in several different ways helps children remember its message. This also allows for the fleshing out of ideas, resulting in learned skills for coping with the common problems and issues of children and adolescence.

You may choose to use one, a few, or all of the topic pages within each chapter. They are designed to motivate children to think about, talk about, and understand the dynamics of the issue presented. Coping skills are incorporated into each topic page, as well as in the activity pages offered at the conclusion of each chapter. Each page contains a limitless number of "story starters," or ideas that will prompt a student to talk about something that happened to him/her, a friend, a loved one, and so on. As other students listen to these stories, they will likely want to tell their own—and so the discussion begins.

The material found in *LIFEWORKS: Behavioral Health in the Classroom* can be used in a group setting or offered to individual students who display behavior indicating a potential problem. From this springboard, students should then be considered for referral to the appropriate professionals in your school or behavioral health facility, to provide the additional support, assistance, and help they need.

Besides providing bottom-line basic facts and sometimes disturbing but vital information, this guidebook will give students a chance to speak their minds. Once they begin, don't try to hold them back! A wise person once said, "If you can feel it, you can heal it." If they are talking, they are feeling. This book results from our desire to help students develop an awareness of their feelings and problems, which is the place from which all healing begins.

Nancy DiNatale
Hennie Shore

TABLE OF CONTENTS

TABLE OF CONTENTS

TABLE OF CONTENTS

TABLE OF CONTENTS

IMPROVING MOTIVATION

Improving Motivation

This chapter describes the concept of motivation. It provides motivational strategies and goal-setting techniques, and points out the benefits of maintaining a positive attitude, including improving homework motivation and getting along with teachers. The chapter concludes with two activity sheets designed to emphasize goal setting and aspects of achievement.

Time Allotment

Two 50-minute sessions integrated into a series of 50-minute class periods.

Goal

To help develop the characteristic of self-motivation, with emphasis on homework, relations with teachers, and learning to set goals.

Objectives

- A student will be able to verbalize the definition of motivation.
- A student will be able to list three strategies to help improve motivation.
- A student will learn seven factors that lead to successful goal setting.
- A student will be able to identify three skills to improve homework and study time.

MOTIVATED PEOPLE

Motivated people have the desire and will to face challenges and overcome them. They work hard and, even if they don't get everything they want, they are often satisfied with what they have achieved. But what motivates them to push on, even in the face of obstacles and negative influences?

• **Motivated people have vision.** They set goals for themselves. They are able to gauge the level of commitment, planning, and follow-through necessary to achieve their goal. Vision doesn't just come to you—you develop it over time, through the people, influences, and events to which you are exposed. It is formed as you learn what brings you personal satisfaction, and it usually changes as your life takes different turns.

• **Motivated people are committed.** After they've formed a vision, they transform it into a mission—a sense of reason and purpose. Their commitment is strong enough to withstand peer pressure and disapproval. They know instinctively that wavering and wandering will bring them harm or personal loss. And when they are able to see the fruits of their labor, their sense of commitment is reinforced.

• **Motivated people have a plan.** This plan is specific, detailed, practical, and realistic. It's a step-by-step formula that gets them where they want to go. People with a definite plan determine priorities (studying early before they get too tired), anticipate problems, expect interruptions and distractions (factoring extra time for phone calls, etc.), and allocate a reasonable amount of time to carry out the plan (setting aside an entire weekend in case the English paper takes longer than anticipated).

• **Motivated people follow through.** This is the final, crucial step toward achievement. Follow-through means that you get the job done, because you've envisioned it, committed to it, and planned for it.

People with a definite plan determine priorities, anticipate problems, expect interruptions and distractions, and allocate a reasonable amount of time to carry out the plan.

Unmotivated people are happy with the status quo, and more than happy to go along with the crowd. If an unmotivated student gets a bad grade, she may get upset, but not upset enough to do anything about it. If she lucks out and gets a better grade than she deserves, she's wildly happy, until the next time, when her lack of effort catches up with her—and it always does.

Lack of motivation and underachievement go hand-in-hand. If a person isn't motivated to achieve, it's a sure bet that she won't accomplish much. Let's look at the previous page's characteristics and apply them to unmotivated students.

Lack of motivation and underachievement go hand-in-hand.

•**Unmotivated people don't have vision.** Without a sense of vision, a student can be easily distracted and manipulated. As she has probably never achieved enough to actually feel good about herself, she naturally does the minimum to get by. There's no evidence to connect hard work with achievement and self-satisfaction.

• **Unmotivated people don't have commitment.** Even when an unmotivated person knows that she has to study for a test, the first distraction that comes along—a friend who says, "Let's get a pizza"—is enough to make her forget all about the exam. Living in the moment is much more rewarding than committing herself to a task, especially when the task is not much fun.

• **Unmotivated people don't have a long-term plan.** An unmotivated person's goal may simply be to sleep late or make sure she gets home in time for dinner. This person may say she plans to study harder, but the plan (which really wasn't a plan at all) usually falls apart because there are no specifics or strategies to ensure that something positive will happen.

• **Unmotivated people don't follow through.** They don't follow through because they never committed in the first place. No one expects much of them, so they don't do much. Certainly, they don't expect much of themselves, and they don't do the world—or themselves—much good at all.

MOTIVATIONAL OBSTACLES

People who are motivated believe in their ability to succeed, and they know from experience that success comes only through hard work. Some people think that motivated people are born that way, and others feel motivation is something you can learn. Psychologists have focused on three strategies that people use to rationalize their behavior related to motivation. Do you recognize yourself in any of them? Do you feel that they are effective?

The self-handicapper. Because she has a fairly low opinion of herself, the self-handicapper creates obstacles to success. She sees herself as barely competent, and tells herself, "Better not try too hard. You're doing fine as you are." In order to maintain her self-esteem, she rarely puts herself out—what if she should fail? Beyond this, she'll convince herself that she really shouldn't study too much, because only nerds do well in school. Sometimes the self-handicapper will spread herself too thin. She'll attempt to do too much, or she'll wait until the last minute to write a report or study. When she gets a poor grade, she blames it on the lack of time. She may also make excuses like "I couldn't find anyone to study with," or "I couldn't study because I was out late last night."

The defensive pessimist. The defensive pessimist sets low expectations for herself so that she can prepare for failure. She tells herself, "I'm going to fail this exam because I'm not good in math." She tells others how poorly prepared she is and how difficult a test was in an effort to justify her insecurities. Then, when she does get a bad grade, she feels justified. The flip side is that she's often motivated by the drive to do better, but even when she studies harder and gets a better grade, she remains pessimistic for the next time.

The self-affirmer. When this person fails, she immediately tells herself "So what if you failed the test. You're good at soccer, you have a great sense of humor, people like you . . . " and so on. To avoid being upset by her lack of achievement, she decides that the standards are too high. If she doesn't have to try as hard, she'll do okay, so she decides not to put forth too much effort. Instead, she works harder to get better at the things she knows she does well and for which she's already received recognition.

The self-handicapper creates obstacles to success.

The defensive pessimist sets low expectations.

The self-affirmer avoids being upset by her lack of achievement.

ARE YOU MOTIVATED FROM WITHIN?

Most successful people are motivated from within themselves. They don't really need external motivators, such as getting paid for good grades, or special favors from teachers. Punishment is also an external motivator: some parents think that if they ground you for getting a D, you'll do better next time. Maybe you will, maybe you won't.

If you're motivated by external things, you'll probably choose the fastest and easiest way to learn, because you know that a reward is waiting for you. But do you really want to just get by? Consider these characteristics of motivated people:

- They enjoy learning for its own sake.
- They love a challenge and will work until they figure out a difficult problem or concept.
- They are curious about different things, and their interest is piqued when they are presented with a new subject.
- They choose to learn about something new instead of going over something they're already familiar with.
- They pursue a topic or think of questions beyond the teacher's requirements.
- They pursue extra projects and opportunities for independent study.
- They love to learn new things.

If you love to learn, you should never be embarrassed or shy about it. Research has found that the most successful achievers are those who have a strong intellectual curiosity. You have the right to have a say in your education, and your education should be meaningful, exciting, and, most of all, fun.

If you feel that you need more challenge in school, talk to your parents and teachers. They will probably be thrilled that you're showing extra interest. Teachers have access to special educational materials that are hard for other people to find, and they can give you extra work and assignments that you can do in your free time. You may even find a teacher who is willing to be your mentor in exploring subjects of shared interest.

Motivated people choose to learn about something new instead of going over something they're already familiar with.

POSITIVE MOTIVATION

You've heard the expression "a positive attitude," but have you ever thought about what it really means? People who have a positive attitude see the glass half full instead of half empty. They believe that a situation will work out, and, if it doesn't, they're still able to see good within the failure.

You can choose to be positive or negative. If you have a positive attitude, you'll be motivated to move onward and upward in every area of your life. Here are some elements of a positive attitude:

• **Being optimistic.** If you feel that something good will happen instead of something bad, your entire sense of well-being will be enhanced. You'll feel ready for anything that may come your way.

• **Accepting things as they are.** Face it—there are some things you can change, and there are a lot of things you can't change. This doesn't mean giving up when things don't go your way. It just means accepting the failure and moving on to the next thing.

• **Being resilient.** Everyone has setbacks—you may get a bad grade, or you may not make a sports team. You may find out that a friend really isn't your friend at all. Being resilient means being able to bounce back and then go forward.

• **Being cheerful.** It's just as easy to say silly, funny, or lighthearted things as it is to badmouth something. If you can see something humorous in a not-so-funny situation, you may find that things are not as bad as they seem.

• **Being enthusiastic.** If you think, "Maybe something great will happen today," you're helping yourself to look forward to whatever happens. If something great doesn't happen, there's always a chance that it will tomorrow.

• **Having a sense of humor.** This is related to being cheerful. If you can make a joke or see something funny in a situation, your world may be brighter. People always like someone who has a sense of humor.

• **Being a good sport.** This attitude can really help, especially when you don't win. Losing isn't usually one person's "fault." Being able to lose gracefully is a skill that will win you friends in the long run.

• **Being hopeful.** Without hope, life has little meaning. Think about what you hope or wish for, and try to formulate a plan to make your hopes and dreams come true.

If you feel that something good will happen instead of something bad, your entire sense of well-being will be enhanced.

If you can make a joke or see something funny in a situation, your world may be brighter.

GOAL SETTING

Part of being a motivated person is setting goals for yourself. If you try to do too much, you'll set yourself up for failure, and if you try to do too little, you'll eventually get into a pattern of underachievement and expecting little from yourself.

In 1944, a psychologist named Kurt Lewin came up with four factors that determine whether a person will succeed or fail. He suggested that a person will experience success if (1) she can define her own goals, (2) these goals are related to her central needs and values, (3) she can define the paths that lead to the accomplishment of the goals, and (4) the goals represent a realistic level of aspiration: neither too high nor too low, but high enough to challenge her capabilities.

Goal-setting guidelines include:

- **Goals must be desirable.** Most importantly, your goal should be something you really want to achieve. This can include things you really don't want to do but know you have to do (such as studying hard to get a good grade).

- **Goals must be conceivable.** When you're thinking about a goal, decide whether it makes sense. Can it be easily understood, imagined, or believed, or is it too hard to achieve?

- **Goals must be believable.** You have to believe that it's possible to attain the goal. If it seems impossible, then it's probably wise not to move toward it.

- **Goals must be controllable.** Think about the factors that might put the goal out of your reach. There will be some things that are out of your control. Will these set you up for failure before you begin?

- **Goals must be measurable.** You need some way of reporting back to yourself whether you've accomplished a step toward your goal.

- **Goals shouldn't be qualified.** This means that each step toward your goal needs to be as important to you as the one before it and the one after it. Every step should be viewed as crucial.

- **Goals should help you grow.** Goals should be positive, so you can build on them in a healthy way. Once you've achieved one goal, your next one can be more challenging and satisfying.

When you're thinking about a goal, decide whether it makes sense.

Goals should be positive, so you can build on them in a healthy way.

HOMEWORK MOTIVATION

Face it—homework is a fact of life. You can make excuses about doing it and you can put if off till midnight, but there's no getting around it. Sooner or later, you have to do it, because if you don't there will be a price to pay.

Believe it or not, there are some very good reasons why teachers give homework, including the fact that it:

- Helps you practice skills that you haven't yet mastered.
- Teaches you how to be responsible.
- Allows you to review skills that you may otherwise forget.
- Prepares you for the next day's lessons.

Here are some tips that will help you get through your homework and studying time more smoothly:

- **Where you study or do your homework is just as important as how you do it.** A good work area is one that is well-lit, free of distractions, quiet, and neat. If you can, designate a space that is only for studying. That way, you'll begin to work as soon as you sit down. Turn off the TV, and close the door. Make sure everything you need is close at hand, and use a chair that supports your back. Facing a blank wall is a good idea so that you won't be distracted by what's happening outside.

- **Plan what you're going to do first, next, and so on.** It's a good idea to visualize your homework in manageable portions. Do the hardest homework first, when your mind is most ready for input. If you have a lot of work, take short breaks between each subject, but don't get distracted.

- **Use the 5R method of studying.** These are Read, Recite, "Rite," Reflect, and Review. First, formulate some questions you have about the subject. Read the material carefully, mentally recite it so that you remember it, and write down what you have read in outline form. Think about the material and decide whether your questions have been answered, and review the material within 24 hours to ensure that you've retained what you've studied.

A good work area is one that is well-lit, free of distractions, quiet, and neat. If you can, designate a space that is only for studying.

MOTIVATION AND TEACHERS

It's really hard to be motivated when you're having a problem with your teacher. Maybe it seems as if everything you do is wrong or maybe she picks on you for no good reason. Maybe the work she gives is way too hard, or her tests are really unfair. Or maybe it just seems as if your teacher is the enemy. Maybe, just maybe, her attitude will change if you are willing to make some changes. This is where motivation on your part comes in.

It's never too late to pay attention, be respectful, and ask questions in class. If you show up for class on time and do your homework, you're one step ahead of the game, and the teacher will notice this. If you study hard, even if you don't do as well as you expected, the teacher will probably know that you put in a lot of effort. If you're unhappy about a bad grade, you can talk to the teacher about it. In fact, you can talk to most teachers about almost anything that's bothering you. You may be surprised how willing she is to help out—and not just with school matters, with personal problems, too.

If you really have a personality conflict with a teacher, you should try to establish a good relationship anyway. Your grade and well-being in class depend on it. Constantly second-guessing a teacher's judgment will not gain you points. And if the teacher finds you annoying, it'll be hard to convince her otherwise when you do change your behavior.

It helps to remember that teachers are people too: If they are new to teaching, it may be doubly hard to keep control and teach at the same time. Job stress, family issues, and health problems are all factors that can make a teacher cranky and irritable. And although you may think that these problems have nothing to do with you, they do—when it comes to your grades and overall school performance.

Do you dislike a particular subject? Wishing you didn't have to take chemistry won't make it go away. Ask yourself, "What can this class do for me, and how can I get along better with this teacher?" The best advice is to try to learn whatever you can, and keep the larger picture in mind: You're building on skills that will help you through college and beyond.

ACTIVITY: MOTIVATION AND GOALS

It's fun to think about what you'd like to do or what you'd like to be someday. Here is a list of goals that affect all parts of your life. Rank them in order, with "1" being most important to you, "2" being somewhat important, and "3" being not very important at all.

___ Being very successful in your profession
___ Being moderately successful in your profession
___ Having a spouse and children
___ Being a good, "hands-on" parent
___ Living in a big city
___ Living in a small town
___ Being well-schooled and knowledgeable about many things
___ Having leisure time to relax and have fun
___ Having a high-paying job
___ Having a job you love that doesn't pay very well
___ Working with people
___ Working at a "desk job" without much contact with others
___ Having a big house with luxuries—pool, tennis court, etc.
___ Having a house that fulfills basic needs
___ Being an entrepreneur (having your own business)
___ Working for someone else and having little responsibility
___ Having the freedom and money to travel and see the world
___ Having close friendships and relationships with family
___ Owning a pet
___ Being famous
___ (Other)
___ (Other)

Now look at the goals you ranked "1," and circle the words that seem to relate to these goals. Think about what will motivate you to achieve your goals.

power   meaning
independence   friendship
love   happiness
security   adventure
excitement   money
prestige   fame
belonging   empathy
comfort   knowledge
truth   challenge

ACTIVITY: I KNOW I CAN DO IT

Motivation goes hand-in-hand with achievement; it's being motivated to do something that gets the momentum going so that you can do it. Having confidence in yourself helps, too. Fill in the blanks with examples of things you want to achieve, obstacles that may be in the way, and ways to combat the doubts you may have.

Here's what I want to do: <u>I want to run for class president.</u>
But I may not be able to achieve my goal because: <u>I'm afraid I won't win, and that I'm not popular enough, and that people won't like my speech, and that I'll make a fool of myself.</u>
I'm going to go for it anyway because: <u>I have the support of my friends and family, most people know I care about school matters, and I really want to be president.</u>

Here's what I want to do: _____

_____

_____

But I may not be able to achieve my goal because: _____

_____

_____

I'm going to go for it anyway because: _____

_____

_____

_____

Here's what I want to do: _____

_____

_____

But I may not be able to achieve my goal because: _____

_____

_____

I'm going to go for it anyway because: _____

_____

_____

_____

SUCCESSFUL RELATIONSHIPS

Successful Relationships

This chapter offers information about the importance of social skills, peer relationships, relationships with parents, body language, and active listening. The chapter focuses on ways to achieve successful relationships by improving social skills. The chapter concludes with activity sheets on active listening and rating relationships.

Time Allotment

Two 50-minute sessions integrated into a series of 50-minute class periods.

Goal

To learn skills that will help students improve the way they interact with others and how they feel about themselves.

Objectives

- A student will be able to verbalize the benefits of having social skills.
- A student will be able to list at least six of the eleven keys to successful relationships.
- A student will learn the four basic levels in establishing a relationship with others.
- A student will be able to identify six factors that influence relations with parents/guardians.
- A student will be able to practice at least five of ten suggestions for improving communication with parents.
- A student will be able to interpret various forms of body language.
- A student will learn two basic concepts of active listening.

THE IMPORTANCE OF SOCIAL SKILLS

Do you get into fights at the drop of a hat? Complain when asked to do something? Lose your temper a lot? Have trouble making and keeping friends?

If you answered yes to most of these questions, it is a good bet that you are lacking in social skills. When used correctly, social skills, or the ability to get along with others in socially acceptable ways, can lead to successful relationships and increased self-esteem. Simply put, having friends, doing things with them, and getting positive feedback from them can help you feel really good about yourself. Social skills can also help you get along better with parents and siblings, teachers, and others.

Activities that many people find quite easy, such as having a conversation or making plans with someone, can present major problems for a young person who has poor social skills or little or no self-confidence. It can also be difficult to behave in a socially acceptable way when you are under stress or you have other significant problems.

People who display aggressive and/or delinquent behavior, who are victims of past or current abuse or neglect, who have mental health problems, who are lonely and have no friends, or who have problems with learning and/or self-control are likely also to have social skills problems. If you have any of these problems, or similar ones, the causes may not be your "fault." Children learn from what they see around them; if the members of your family do not get along with each other, chances are your relationships with others will suffer too.

But the good news is that social skills can be learned, and it is never too late to learn them. There are specific steps that can be practiced (which we discuss later in this chapter), but ultimately it is up to you to decide whether you want to make the effort.

Remember, having and keeping friends is often hard work. You may befriend someone whom you later decide isn't your kind of person at all. A friend may do something that really makes you angry, and you have to decide whether to work things out or move on. One thing's for sure, though—real friends are always worth having and keeping.

The good news is that social skills can be learned, and it is never too late to learn them.

Making friends is hard work, but there are specific ways to do it. Here are some tried-and-true strategies:

1. Reach out. If you think you'd like to get to know someone, don't wait for him to make the first move. If you smile and say "Hi," you'll be on your way.

2. Show interest. Don't just talk about yourself; ask questions and comment on the answers.

3. Be a good listener. Look at the person who is talking to you. Pay attention to what's being said rather than thinking about what you're going to say next.

4. Open up. When you've given the other person a chance, tell about yourself.

5. Don't brag. Talk about your skills and accomplishments with some modesty. Nobody likes a show-off.

6. Be honest. Tell the truth. Never make things up or exaggerate. You'll be found out eventually. Be honest in your opinions, but be discreet.

7. Be diplomatic. This means deciding whether it's worth taking a risk by "telling it like it is." Sometimes being diplomatic is the better course. For example, if you don't like someone's clothes, it's better not to comment than to tell the truth.

8. Don't just dump. Real friends are there for you through good as well as bad times. But new friends may be turned off if everything you say is negative.

9. Do your share. Every relationship takes work. The give-and-take in any friendship involves contact, planning, and follow-through. Don't depend on the other person to do this when you're not doing your part.

10. Be accepting. Not everyone has to think and act exactly like you. Some of the best friends you'll find may be very different from you.

11. Get involved. Join groups, clubs, teams—anything that will give you opportunities to interact with kids your age. An added bonus is that these kids already have something in common with you.

Don't just talk about yourself; ask questions and comment on the answers.

Every relationship takes work. The give-and-take in any friendship involves contact, planning, and follow-through.

PEER RELATIONSHIPS

How strong are your peer relationships (relationships with equals, with others of your own age)? Do you have many friends or just a few? Are you popular, in the "in crowd"? Or do you have very few friends? Do you feel left out on the fringe of activities? Do you prefer to stay home alone to avoid feeling lonely in a crowd?

Close peer relationships do not just happen. They are built over time and depend on mutual trust and support. Without these, they don't last. Here are some factors that come into play in peer relationships:

• People are liked and become popular when they are cooperative and friendly in their peer interactions. They are disliked and rejected when they are aggressive or disruptive in their interactions with others.

• People who are constantly teased, excluded, or bullied contribute to these responses through their own behavior. Their social inabilities are often a trigger of the poor relationship, and these inabilities result in poor self-esteem, so that the individuals begin to feel that they deserve what they get.

• As a result of these negative reactions, these people sometimes turn out to be bullies themselves, finding comfort in putting others down. Sometimes they find it easier to befriend the bully and become his side-kick. Or they choose to turn completely inward, avoiding contact with others.

• People who reveal too much about themselves before they've developed trusting relationships (or before they're reasonably sure that others like them) risk being rejected.

• Trust is the basis of sharing in relationships. The better you know and trust someone, the more you are willing to share with him, and vice versa.

Close peer relationships do not just happen. They are built over time and depend on mutual trust and support.

Have you heard the expression "A friend is a present you give yourself?" If you have good friends, you know what this means. If you don't, you may need to try harder to build relationships with your peers.

Trust is the basis of sharing in relationships. The better you know and trust someone, the more you are willing to share with him, and vice versa. Consider the elements of trust as you think about your friendships and relationships:

Surface relationships are about basic facts. These relationships are those you have with classmates and other people you don't know very well. You share safe, non-threatening, non-personal information with these people, such as homework or activity schedules. There's little or nothing going on beyond the information.

By revealing your opinions and feelings, you show yourself to others. You also set yourself up for disagreements, disappointments, being perceived as "different," and possible rejection.

"Get to know me" relationships are about what you think. "I like that CD." "Her hair looks horrible." "Mrs. B. is so unfair!" Here risk and trust begin to surface. By revealing your opinions and feelings, you show yourself to others. You also set yourself up for disagreements, disappointments, being perceived as "different," and possible rejection. At the same time, you begin to let people know who you are and what is important to you.

More trusting relationships are about feelings. In these relationships, you are beyond the point of thinking before you offer a compliment, comfort, a hug, or a gift. For example, your best friend breaks up with her boyfriend, so you comfort her. Another friend gets a bad grade, so you offer your help in the future. Feelings are experienced and shared, and the participants are vulnerable. This requires a lot of trust, and the assurance that the people with whom you share won't make fun of you or desert you when you need them.

The most trusting relationships are about your feelings for the other person. In these you share your love, hurt, anger, happiness, admiration, disappointment, and so on. These exchanges involve disclosure, great risk, mutual trust and deep sharing. Have you ever heard someone talk about two friends who haven't seen each other in years, but feel as though they were never apart when they finally do reunite? These relationships continue to grow stronger and often last for a long time, even if the friends hardly ever see each other.

RELATIONSHIPS WITH PARENTS

Parents and teens often experience conflict. Parents may have a hard time accepting that their children are becoming adults, and they may continue to treat them like children. As teens become independent, they want their own maturity to be recognized. Part of being a teen is developing your own identity, being independent from your parents. So teens often find it difficult to believe that when parents impose curfews and limitations, they are usually doing it out of love and concern.

Parents and teenagers often have differing views on responsibility, as well as different worries and life values. An inability to communicate effectively can make the situation seem almost hopeless.

One way to get along with your parents is to try to understand these differences. Since parents are less likely to change, it may be up to you to cultivate a better relationship. But first you have to understand the reasons for their actions. Consider these issues:

• **Power and control.** Because they are older and have had much more experience, parents often think that dominating their children is the same as guiding them through life. They feel it is their job to do this. But as they dominate you, you feel trapped.

• **Your choice of friends.** This may be a real bone of contention. If your parents don't like your friends, then they don't have to spend time with them, right? Be honest, and ask yourself whether they're just being parents or whether they have a point. Are you hanging out with a bunch of losers just to spite your parents? Did you choose these friends just because they accepted you?

• **Trust.** Parents lose trust when you break the rules. Trust can also be lost when communication breaks down and when assumptions are made. The best way to keep your parents' trust is to follow the rules and talk to them—if you did something wrong, tell them why you did it, and go from there. Don't always assume your parents will react negatively.

• **Opinions.** Your opinions are just that—yours—and no one should belittle them. Parents sometimes fail to realize this, thinking their opinion is better than yours, just because they're older and supposedly wiser.

• **Values.** Chances are, your values are the ones your parents taught you when you were a kid, but they've changed just a bit to suit your new identity. Try to explain the changes to your parents. Give them a chance to listen. Just the fact that you care enough to explain should make them respect you for the person you've become.

Parental pride. Parents are often obsessed with how much they have done for you. This makes them feel entitled to your obedience and appreciation.

A survey of teenagers revealed this enlightening result: When asked what they want from their parents, the majority said, "We want them to listen to us." One student said, "Just talk to me . . . Make time in your busy schedule to learn more about me."

To get your parents to learn more about you, you may need to take the initiative. If you can tell people what you want and need, in a way that enables them to really hear what you are saying, you'll be successful in achieving many of your goals. Parents are no different, even though it may seem that they are always on the opposite side. If you can make them listen, not only will your relationship with them change for the better, you'll get more of what you want. Consider these suggestions:

- **Choose your time wisely.** Make an appointment to talk. Don't start a serious discussion when your parents are tired, stressed out, or busy.

- **Be respectful.** Parents are much more willing to listen when they don't feel as if they're being attacked. Think about it: Aren't you being aggressive?

- **Choose your words wisely.** Say what you mean and don't take forever to say it. Be concise and precise.

- **Bring suggestions to the discussion.** Make a list of possible solutions to the problem, and get your parents to help you choose the best one.

- **Make an effort to see their point of view.** Remember, they have your best interests at heart. They care about you—you're their child. Listen to their thoughts and opinions, and reflect on them.

- **Watch your body language.** Rolling your eyes, turning your back, walking away . . . none of these will help to get the problem solved.

- **Don't yell or be belligerent.** Nobody likes to be put down.

- **Use "I" statements.** Instead of "You never let me do anything," try "I feel like you don't trust me to make my own decisions."

- **Pay attention.** Look at your parents while they're speaking, and ask them to do the same for you.

- **Compromise.** You may get even more than you bargained for!

Don't start a serious discussion when your parents are tired, stressed out, or busy.

Parents are much more willing to listen when they don't feel as if they're being attacked.

THE GIVE-AND-TAKE OF RELATIONSHIPS

Friendships are circular: one friend gives, the other takes and gives back, then the cycle repeats itself. When you make yourself available to others, you get good things in return:

• **You get in touch with your true feelings.** We often have conflicting thoughts and feelings, and when we talk about them to a friend, this enables us to form an opinion or make a decision. Saying something out loud to a person you trust is very satisfying.

• **You hone your communication skills.** The more you share your feelings, the better you get at recognizing and describing them. When you're feeling sad, or angry, or any negative feeling, you have someone to talk to and the tools to verbalize your feelings. In this way you can get the help and support you need.

• **You learn the joys of trusting others.** When you communicate positively with others, they respond to you in the same manner. Try telling someone how you feel about something. The conversation will help you sort things out, and soon that person will probably tell you how he feels about it. You get the person's perspective and he gets yours. You learn to trust each other in solving problems.

• **You discover that you're not alone.** The more you share, the more you'll find that everyone has similar fears, problems, and situations.

• **You get to vent.** Once you trust someone, you'll be able to release stress by talking to him about your frustrations and problems. The give-and-take of the discussion and the ability to see a problem from more than one perspective will help you calm down.

• **You become strong enough to consider criticism.** Your relationship is solid enough for the other person to tell you if he thinks you are wrong, and you can consider what is actually being said rather than feeling hurt or attacked.

Saying something out loud to a person you trust is very satisfying.

BODY LANGUAGE

Sometimes it's not what you say, it's the way you appear to others when you say it. Take a look at yourself right now. Are your hands open or closed? Are your arms crossed in front of your body? Are you leaning forward, eager to hear what's being said, or are you slumped back, looking like you couldn't care less?

These actions are non-verbal signals. They are what your facial expressions, gestures, posture, and eye contact tell the world about you. They tell people how you really feel about a situation. Likewise, you can tell how others feel by watching their body language. Look for these signs:

- Cocking the head to one side suggests uncertainty.

- Crossing your arms is a basic way you protect yourself against threats, whether they are real or imagined.

- Covering your mouth suggests that you're trying to hide your expression, or you're trying not to let your thoughts leak out.

- Pressing your lips together shows annoyance and an attempt to hide anger. Biting your lips can mean you're tense or nervous.

- Leaning your head in your hand suggests boredom. Putting your hands behind your head suggests uncertainty and stress.

- Open arms suggest warmth and openness. Tilting the head along with open arms suggests closeness and comfort.

- Mirroring someone's posture shows you're at ease with him.

- Toes pointed inward suggest submission. Toes pointed out mean you're in control.

- Clenched hands suggest defensiveness and an attempt to keep control.

- Mutual staring can mean strong attraction, or the exact opposite.

- A hand on your hip suggests assertiveness, as does facing a person directly while talking to him.

- Facing a person squarely also communicates your involvement in what he is saying.

- Positioning yourself at an appropriate distance from the speaker—allowing him personal space—means that you are an attentive listener.

Leaning your head in your hand suggests boredom.

ACTIVITY: ACTIVE LISTENING

There are many ways to show people you care about them. Listening, really hearing what a person is saying, and not just agreeing, is one way. In order to communicate, you have to be very skilled at listening. You have to let the person know that you hear what is being said.

Active listening teaches you how to let other people know that you really understand. If you can become an active listener, you'll have more friends and stronger relationships. Two basic concepts of active listening are mirroring and clarifying.

1. In mirroring, you actually mirror what the other person is feeling:

"You sound (<u>feeling</u>) about (<u>situation</u>)."
  or
"You must really feel _____."
  or
"What you're saying is that _____."

2. In clarifying, you actually ask the person to explain the situation:

"So what happened that got you so upset?"
 or
"What happened next?"

Fill in these active listening blanks:

"You can't trust anyone without getting stabbed in the back!"
    You sound _____.
    What happened that made you so _____?

"School is stupid. I'm never going back there. Who needs it?"
    Did something happen at _____? What was it?
    You sound_____ about _____.

"Nobody cares about me, so why should I talk about my problems?"
    You seem _____.
    Who doesn't care about you?

"I'm such a loser. I can't do anything right."
    What happened to make you feel so _____?
    You seem so _____. Tell me about it.

"What if I make a fool of myself?"
    You seem _____. Is that how you feel?
    Why do you feel so _____?

How are your peer relationships? Are you doing all you can to keep them strong and healthy? Don't assume that friends are friends forever. If you don't work on your friendships, you may find yourself with no friends at all. The following statements will help you determine whether you are a true friend or just an acquaintance.

	NEVER	SOMETIMES	OFTEN
I call my friend on the phone just to talk.	☐	☐	☐
I ask my friend's opinion on an issue.	☐	☐	☐
I trust my friend with my secret(s).	☐	☐	☐
I tell my friend when he/she hurts me.	☐	☐	☐
I give my friend a compliment.	☐	☐	☐
I listen when a friend needs to talk.	☐	☐	☐
I don't listen to rumors about my friend.	☐	☐	☐
If I think he/she's wrong, I tell him/her.	☐	☐	☐
I defend my friend against bullies.	☐	☐	☐
I ask for his/her support/understanding.	☐	☐	☐
I tell my friend how I feel about him/her.	☐	☐	☐
I do something nice "just because."	☐	☐	☐
I tell him/her he/she's important to me.	☐	☐	☐
I suggest things we can do together.	☐	☐	☐
I show my friend respect and kindness.	☐	☐	☐
I don't try to change his/her opinions.	☐	☐	☐
I stick up for him/her.	☐	☐	☐
I'm there for my friend when needed.	☐	☐	☐
I do something he/she really wants to do,	☐	☐	☐

even if it doesn't interest me.

INCREASING SELF-ESTEEM

Increasing Self-Esteem

This chapter reviews the concept of self-esteem. It describes ways to challenge self-defeating thoughts and provides tools to help boost a person's self-concept. The activity sheets focus on learning about ways we think and feel and how our thoughts influence our self-esteem.

Time Allotment

Two 50-minute sessions integrated into a series of 50-minute class periods.

Goals

To identify factors that influence the way people feel about themselves. To learn skills and tools to help improve the concept of self-esteem.

Objectives

- A student will be able to verbalize factors that affect levels of self-esteem.
- A student will learn nine ways to identify and challenge self-defeating thoughts.
- A student will be able to identify messages learned in childhood and understand how these messages influence self-esteem.
- A student will be able to identify at least six coping skills to increase self-esteem.

WHAT IS SELF-ESTEEM?

Self-esteem is the confidence and satisfaction you have in yourself. It comes from being aware of what is important to you, achieving goals and meeting expectations, and taking responsibility for your actions. It also comes from:

- Love, respect, and acceptance
- Being listened to and being taken seriously
- Having your needs met
- Being honored for your individuality
- Being able to talk to yourself in a positive way
- Being healthy and fit
- Having a sense of purpose in life
- Having a sense of humor, laughter, and the ability to be playful
- Taking pride in your cultural heritage
- Being able to make choices and having a sense of personal power
- Relying on your judgment and personal values
- Feeling safe and secure
- Doing good for others
- Being competent and able to achieve

Factors that contribute to low self-esteem include:

- Being rejected and put down
- Lack of previous successes
- Lack of faith in your judgment
- Disrespect from others
- Having parents with low self-esteem
- Reluctance to try new things

Individuals with low self-esteem feel:

- Isolated and unlovable
- Unable to express their needs and feelings
- Afraid to confront their problems
- A lack of faith in themselves
- Undeserving of anything better than what they already have
- Deserving of rejection and failure
- Unable to do anything to improve their situation

WHEN YOU FEEL LIKE A FAILURE

You're not a failure if you need time to reach your goal — you're just human like everyone else.

A mistake is not a failure. No one does everything perfectly.

Sometimes when you try to do something and it doesn't work out, it feels like nothing is right. Feelings of failure can really hurt, but they can also help you in the long run. Think about this quote from Robert F. Kennedy: "Those who dare to fail miserably can achieve greatly." Here are some things to ask yourself when things go wrong:

• **Was your goal reasonable?** When the goal is achievable, and when it means something to you to achieve it (rather than pleasing someone else by doing it), you're much more likely to succeed at it. Sometimes goals take lots of time and effort to achieve. You're not a failure if you need time to reach your goal—you're just human like everyone else.

• **Would your best friend say you're a failure?** Would you say your best friend was a failure in the same situation? Probably not. You may be much kinder to others than you are to yourself. Give yourself a break and treat yourself as well as you treat your friends.

• **Do you overuse the word "failure?"** Do you feel that if you don't do everything perfectly, you're automatically a failure? A mistake is not a failure. No one does everything perfectly. What counts is making the effort, trying to do something, taking a risk.

• **How can failure be a benefit?** It may bring some good things your way. For example, if you fail a music competition, it could make your parents understand they should never have forced you to take piano lessons in the first place. Failure can also make you realize that you're trying to do too much at one time.

• **When are you responsible for failures?** Sometimes failure is out of your control—such as when you lose an election or flunk a test because you had a family emergency and couldn't study. But sometimes things are in your control. Does your teacher have it in for you because you are the class clown or because you're not trying hard enough? Changing your behavior can lessen your chances of failing.

• **What can you learn from your failures?** Everything in life is an experience, and even negative experiences can teach you something. You may learn that a certain activity isn't for you, or that you should have prepared better for it. Hopefully, you'll learn that you can survive setbacks and disappointments much better than you ever thought you could.

CHALLENGING SELF-DEFEATING THOUGHTS

When we assume certain things about ourselves and others, we're often wrong. Our assumptions may be based on false facts. Self-defeating thoughts are just that—self-defeating. They put you down in your own mind, and they make you feel bad. And much of the time, they're wrong! Ask yourself these questions when you're feeling unsure:

Am I overgeneralizing?
- I didn't get a good grade, therefore I'll never get a good grade in the future, no matter what I do.
- I didn't make the team, so that means I should never try out for a sport again.

Am I labeling and/or mislabeling?
- My brother said I'm a loser and he must be right.
- I'm so stupid because I never get my homework done on time.

Am I reasoning with my emotions instead of my mind?
- I think my boss is unhappy with my work, so I'm probably going to get fired.
- My father thinks I can't do anything right, so I know he doesn't love me.

Am I jumping to conclusions?
- I wasn't invited to the party because no one likes me.
- My mother is going to freak out because I forgot to buy milk.

Am I engaging in all-or-nothing thinking?
- I didn't get an A, so I may as well have failed.
- If I can't have the car, I won't be able to get anywhere.

Am I catastrophizing?
- I missed the class, and I'll never be able to make it up.
- I get teased in school, and I'll never be able to make friends.

Am I "shoulding" myself to death?
- I should understand this homework.
- I should be taking care of my mother instead of having fun with my friends.

Do I disregard the positive?
- I got an A, but so did everyone else.
- The teacher asked for my help, but she chose someone else yesterday.

Am I personalizing events?
- If I'd studied harder, my mother wouldn't have gotten sick.
- If I'd caused less trouble, my parents wouldn't have got divorced.

SELF-ESTEEM BUSTERS AND BUILDERS

There are many messages we give and receive as we go through our lives. When you think about it, it's surprising how many of these messages are negative and "esteem-busting."

These messages sometimes result from comparing ourselves to others. There will always be people who are better looking, smarter, richer, and just plain luckier. That's life, so what's the point of being jealous?

People tend to think things like "I'm so fat that no one will ever want me" or "I'm too stupid to get into college." It's unfortunate that most people have to remind themselves to focus on their good qualities, to look on the bright side of life. Here's how to do it:

Instead of thinking...	*Try thinking...*
"I'm too emotional."	"I'm aware of my feelings."
"I'm too shy."	"I'm thoughtful and quiet."
"I'm too fat."	"I like myself the way I am."
"I'm too pushy."	"I know how to get things done."
"I'm too skinny."	"I'm built like my dad."
"I'm ugly."	"I may not be gorgeous, but I'm okay."
"I'm too nosy."	"I love learning new things."
"I care too much."	"I care about people's feelings."
"I make too many mistakes."	"I keep trying to get it right."
"I try too hard."	"I want things to turn out right."
"I'm too cautious."	"I think before I act."
"I'm too tall."	"I'm built like my mom."
"I'm too sloppy."	"I like things to be informal."
"I'm too silly."	"I love to have fun."
"I'm too sensible."	"I like things to make sense."
"I'm too smart."	"I love to learn."
"I'm not fun enough."	"People like me for other reasons."
"I'm not smart enough."	"I may not get As, but I do okay."
"I'm not pretty enough."	"I have my own look."
"I'm not strong enough."	"I'm strong enough for other things."
"I'm not fast enough."	"I'll try something else."
"I'm not good enough."	"I am good enough."

YOUR POSITIVE QUALITIES

In order to help increase self-esteem, it is important to first take a look at all the positive qualities that we possess. Circle all that apply.

ABLE
ACCEPTING
ADAPTABLE
ADVENTUROUS
AFFECTIONATE
AMBITIOUS
ARTISTIC
ASSERTIVE
ATTRACTIVE
BOLD
BROAD-MINDED
CANDID
CAPABLE
CAREFUL
CARING
CAUTIOUS
CHARMING
CHEERFUL
CLEAR-THINKING
CLEVER
COMPASSIONATE
COMPETENT
CONFIDENT
CONSCIENTIOUS
CONSIDERATE
COOPERATIVE
COURAGEOUS
CREATIVE
CURIOUS
DEPENDABLE
DETERMINED
DYNAMIC
EAGER
EASY-GOING
EFFICIENT
EMPATHIC
ENERGETIC
ENTERPRISING
ENTHUSIASTIC
FAIR-MINDED
FAITHFUL
FIT

FLEXIBLE
FORGIVING
FRIENDLY
FUNNY
GENEROUS
GENTLE
GOOD-NATURED
HAPPY
HEALTHY
HELPFUL
HONEST
HOPEFUL
HUMOROUS
IDEALISTIC
IMAGINATIVE
INDEPENDENT
INDIVIDUALISTIC
INDUSTRIOUS
INTELLIGENT
INVENTIVE
KIND
LIGHT-HEARTED
LIKABLE
LOGICAL
LOVABLE
LOVING
MATURE
MERRY
MILD
MODEST
NATURAL
NEAT
NURTURING
OPEN-MINDED
OPTIMISTIC
ORGANIZED
ORIGINAL
OUTGOING
PATIENT
PEACE-LOVING
PERSISTENT
PLEASANT

POLITE
POSITIVE
PRACTICAL
PRECISE
PROGRESSIVE
PUNCTUAL
QUIET
RATIONAL
REALISTIC
REASONABLE
RELAXED
RELIABLE
RESOURCEFUL
RESPONSIBLE
SENSIBLE
SEXY
SINCERE
SOCIABLE
SPECIAL
SPONTANEOUS
SPUNKY
STABLE
STRONG
TACTFUL
TALENTED
TOLERANT
TRUSTING
TRUSTWORTHY
UNDERSTANDING
UNIQUE
WARM
WITTY
ZANY

"I SHOULD, NO MATTER WHAT"

Think of something that you'd like to achieve. Would you like to make the team, get better grades, be chosen for a part in the school play? Now think about why this goal is so important to you. Are you doing it for yourself, or are you trying to please someone else because it's what you **should** do? Will it make you happier, or are you doing it for someone else?

Bombarding yourself with "shoulds" will get you nowhere. You don't have to please anyone but yourself and people you really care about. People who try to please everyone end up pleasing no one.

Contemplate these "shoulds," putting "no matter what" after each one, and think about how silly they are:

I should be getting much better grades, *no matter what . . .*

I should be the best child in the world, *no matter what . . .*

I should always get my work done on time, *no matter what . . .*

I should never make any mistakes, *no matter what . . .*

I should always know what to do, *no matter what . . .*

I should always make the right decisions, *no matter what . . .*

I should always feel enthusiastic and energetic, *no matter what . . .*

I should always win arguments with everyone, *no matter what . . .*

I should always do the right thing, *no matter what . . .*

I should know what to do in any situation, *no matter what . . .*

I should always push myself harder, *no matter what . . .*

I should always be on top of a situation, *no matter what . . .*

I should do things I really don't want to do, *no matter what . . .*

I should be strong and face difficulties by myself, *no matter what . . .*

I should always solve another person's problems, *no matter what . . .*

I should never ask for help, *no matter what . . .*

> Bombarding yourself with "shoulds" will get you nowhere. You don't have to please anyone but yourself and people you really care about.

LIFE'S NEGATIVE MESSAGES

Children learn what they see and believe what they're told. The messages our parents and others give us when we're children often become integrated into our lives. Many of these messages become part of us—we hear them and we react—even though they aren't true. Consider these messages, the thoughts and results they trigger, and the "better" messages:

Message: *Boys don't cry.*
Thought: I feel so sad, but everyone will think I'm a wimp if I cry, so I have to hold it in. I can't let my feelings show.
Result: Anger and sadness, which can lead to aggressiveness and other negative behaviors.
Better message: *Everyone cries when they feel sad. It helps them feel better.*

Message: *If something is worth doing, it's worth doing well.*
Thought: I'd better do this right the first time.
Result: Frustration and embarrassment when something is just too hard to do the first try, and reluctance to try again.
Better message: *If something is worth doing, go ahead and try it. If it doesn't work, try again if you want to.*

Message: *To be your best, you must look your best.*
Thought: I must take care to have a perfect appearance, or people won't think I'm worthy.
Result: A false belief that appearance is more important than what is underneath.
Better message: *Doing a good job has nothing to do with your appearance.*

Message: *Let me do it for you. I can do it better.*
Thought: Of course he/she can do it better. I was stupid to think I should even try.
Result: Incompetence and dependence on others when it comes to doing important things.
Better message: *If you can't do something yourself, ask for help.*

Message: *Don't worry, everything will turn out fine.*
Thought: I guess that's right. I was dumb to worry about it.
Result: A false belief that things will be okay when there's a good chance that they won't, and an inability to deal with consequences because you didn't expect them to happen.
Better message: *Sometimes things are not fine, but with time, things could get better.*

Message: *If you ask me one more time, you'll go to your room.*
Thought: My wants and needs are not important.
Result: Shame and loneliness as the result of not being heard or validated.
Better message: *I'm happy to discuss the matter with you in a rational manner.*

Message:
Children should be seen and not heard.
Thought:
I must act like a perfect angel. If I say or do anything, I'd better not mess up.
Result:
Fear of getting in trouble, even for an innocent mistake.
Better message:
If you have something worthy to say, go ahead and say it.

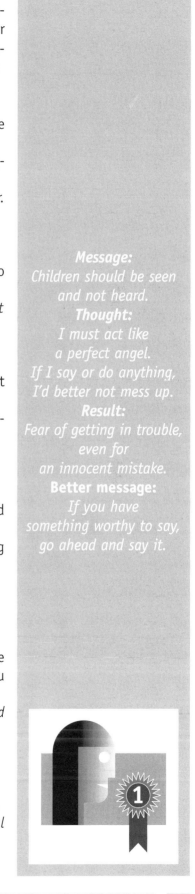

You, and only you, are in control of your self-esteem. Here are some tools to help you:

• **Broadcast your dreams.** No one will know what you want to do unless you tell them. This doesn't mean bragging; it means finding people who can help you achieve your goals and pursuing them.

• **Keep yourself in good shape.** Your body is the only vehicle you have to carry you through life, so take care of it. The world is full of unhealthy temptations: it's up to you to make the right choices and treat your body with respect.

• **Take care of your self-esteem.** A wise person once said "Next to your life, your self-esteem is your most precious possession." It's your measurement of self-worth, and you can see yourself as being worth five dollars, a million dollars, or priceless.

• **Choose your friends wisely.** Choose friends who care about you, share your values and key interests, support your growth and development, and are goal-oriented. These are the friends who will boost your sense of self-worth.

• **Consider the source of advice.** When someone advises you, think first about these things: How does this person live his life? Does he make responsible decisions? Does he have my best interests at heart? Make sure your decisions are your own.

• **Be a leader.** Leaders do things because they want to, not because the group tells them to. Their actions are guided by good values and principles, and their decisions enrich rather than hinder them. Resist negative peer pressure at all costs. Go along with friends only if you want to.

• **Learn how to be alone.** Giving yourself space is giving yourself a gift. You can get to know yourself through doing solitary things, like reading, listening to music, going for a walk alone, and so on.

• **Pay your dues, respectfully.** There's a lot you have to learn while working toward your goals. There will be plenty of people to answer to, but if you keep your ears and eyes open, and learn all you can, you'll no longer be the apprentice, you'll become an expert.

• **Make doors open for you.** Get a job, a hobby, or do community work in your free time. Every new experience can teach you something.

• **Grow through your problems.** You will never be able to avoid problems and challenges, so learn to grow with them. You'll get better at solving them as new ones come along.

ACTIVITY: SELF-ESTEEM WORKSHEET

Fill out this sheet honestly, and think about your answers. Use the back of the sheet if necessary.

I am a _____ person.

My greatest strength is _____.

When I'm angry I usually _____.

When I'm happy I usually _____.

I like to spend my free time _____.

This gives me satisfaction because _____.

Most people think that I'm _____.

Someday I hope to become _____.

When I'm upset I usually _____.

My friends say that I'm _____.

One thing I'm proud of doing is _____.

I'm happiest when _____.

What makes me angry is _____.

Someone I'd like to be like is _____,

because _____.

Something I would love to do is _____.

If I could, I'd change _____.

The hardest thing for me is _____.

I'd love to _____.

I wish I could _____.

I'm at my best when _____.

I wish I could improve my _____.

Something nobody knows about me is _____.

ACTIVITY: DO YOU HAVE LOW SELF-ESTEEM?

Do you see yourself as a failure? Do you expect to fail, and act in ways that sabotage success? Chances are you have low self-esteem. Answer TRUE or FALSE to these questions. If you have fewer true than false answers, you have low self-esteem.

TRUE   FALSE

☐ ☐ I generally feel as competent as my peers.

☐ ☐ I usually feel I can achieve whatever I want.

☐ ☐ What happens to me is mostly in my hands.

☐ ☐ I rarely worry about how things will work out.

☐ ☐ I feel confident that I can deal with most situations.

☐ ☐ I rarely doubt my ability to solve problems.

☐ ☐ I rarely have trouble asking others to do things for me.

☐ ☐ I'm rarely upset by criticism.

☐ ☐ I feel confident about my abilities even when I fail.

☐ ☐ I'm optimistic about my future.

☐ ☐ I feel that I have a lot to offer.

☐ ☐ When I have a setback, I rarely dwell on it.

☐ ☐ I'm always comfortable disagreeing with authority.

☐ ☐ I rarely feel that I'd like to be someone else.

☐ ☐ If I make a mistake, I try again.

☐ ☐ I do things that help me feel good about myself.

☐ ☐ I trust my own judgment.

☐ ☐ I like doing things for the benefit of others.

☐ ☐ It's important to me to be healthy and fit.

☐ ☐ I rarely feel that I should do things differently.

☐ ☐ I rarely look on the negative side of things.

DEALING WITH ANGER

Dealing with Anger

This chapter provides an overview of anger. It defines what anger is and is not. It looks at anger as a secondary emotion. It describes how we can recognize when we are feeling angry and the behaviors associated with this powerful emotion. Coping skills are offered throughout the chapter by helping to identify anger personalities, learning to defuse anger, identifying anger at ourselves, and dealing with another person's anger. A checklist for hidden anger and an exercise on helping to deal with anger constructively are offered at the conclusion of the chapter.

Time Allotment

Two 50-minute sessions integrated into a series of 50-minute class periods.

Goal

To learn ways to deal with anger constructively.

Objectives

- A student will be able to answer the question "What is anger?"
- A student will learn to recognize his associated reactions and behaviors when he is feeling angry.
- A student will be able to identify his "anger personality."
- A student will be able to identify five coping skills to manage anger effectively.

WHAT IS ANGER?

Anger is a natural, human feeling or emotion that everyone experiences. Anger is neither good nor bad. It is the expression of anger that can be harmful or useful, depending what you do with it.

Anger is a warning signal that something is wrong or that a problem exists. It is usually a defense against something, a reaction to hurt, loss, or fear. Anger is our response to an underlying feeling. This feeling is usually fear.

John Anthony Bochnowicz, director of SAFE-Bucks County Peace Center, describes how fear relates to anger:

"When we are in situations that we respond to in a negative manner, these situations have an impact on us that affects the physical, emotional, and spiritual levels. How these situations impact us is determined by our thoughts. Our thoughts determine our feelings, which determine our attitude, which determines our experience. We need to be careful not to allow yesterday's negative experience to become a cause for negative, fearful thoughts today."

In other words, dealing with the cause of your anger as it occurs will prevent "anger spillover" into other interactions that follow.

Mr. Bochnowicz also says, "If you plant a tomato seed, it is not going to grow into an ear of corn. It is going to grow into a tomato plant. If you are having negative fearful thoughts, they are not going to develop into positive loving experiences: they are going to become negative fearful situations. If you want loving experiences, you need to make sure you are having positive, loving thoughts.

Fear is the absence of love. Fear is a dark room, absent of light. If you bring a candle of light into a dark room the darkness disappears. If you bring love into a fearful situation the fear disappears. The pain of fear can be so overwhelming that you do not know what to do with it."

In situations where you experience feelings of fear, you may turn that fear into feelings of anger. The pain gets so intense that you turn it into anger either at yourself or toward others.

Here are other thoughts and facts about anger:

• Anger is a secondary emotion. The primary feeling is usually the feeling of fear. We often use our angry feelings as an emergency escape.

Anger is a warning signal that something is wrong or that a problem exists.

(continued)

(continued)

• There's a difference between anger and aggression, which is an attempt to hurt someone or destroy something, and a violation of the rights of another person.

• You feel angry when you're not getting something you want, when you're frustrated, when your feelings are hurt or misunderstood, when you're unable to do something that you want to do.

• Anger carries a sense of personal violation. When you're angry, you believe that you're right and the other person is wrong.

• When you're angry, it's hard to see the "big picture." Your attention is focused on the cause of the anger instead of what led up to it.

• If you hold your anger in and/or deny it, it can cause anxiety and depression, and it can interfere with your relationships.

• "Dumping," or projecting your anger onto something or someone who is not related to the cause of your anger, may relieve your tension, but it will not solve the problem that made you angry.

• The ability to accept the fact that you're angry, and to feel the anger, is the first step toward redirecting your angry feelings.

• Most of the time, the things and people that make you angry are those you care about the most. Otherwise, you probably wouldn't react in such a passionate manner.

• When used in a positive way, anger can help you make changes in yourself or your environment. It can lead to better understanding. When used in a negative way, it can frighten, intimidate, and isolate you from others.

• Learning to trust yourself and having compassion for others are the best tools for controlling anger.

Most of the time, the things and people that make you angry are those you care about the most.

RECOGNIZING REACTIONS AND BEHAVIORS

There are many human emotions. Anger is one of the strongest and most recognizable. If you know how your body and mind react when you get angry, you can learn how to keep your anger from getting out of control.

When you get angry, you may feel:

Hurt/in pain

Afraid/fearful

Abandoned

Powerless

Worthless

Guilty

Disappointed

Rejected

Like a failure

Sad

Insulted

Ignored/unwanted

Unloved

Unrecognized

When you get angry, you may experience:

Muscular tension

A hot or red face

Sweaty palms

Shakiness

Headache

Stomachache

Dizziness

Increased blood pressure

Faster heartbeat

Rapid breathing

Tense jaw

When you get angry, you may become:

Quiet and withdrawn

Isolated from others

Tearful

Sarcastic and belligerent

Aggressive

Self-critical

Verbally hostile

Physically hostile

Violent

Destructive

Determined to seek revenge

Loud and obnoxious

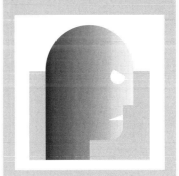

(continued)

(continued)

When you get angry, you may think:

"How dare she!"

"That jerk! I'll fix him!"

"Nobody understands me."

"I'm not going to take it anymore!"

"It doesn't matter."

"It's what I deserve."

"I hate her."

"It's all his fault."

"She's dead wrong."

"Why me?"

"This is so unfair."

"Nobody cares about me."

MANAGING ANGER CONSTRUCTIVELY

Being open, honest, and direct is the most effective way of expressing your anger. This is often difficult, however, because when you're confronting the source of your anger your emotions sometimes get the best of you. You want to appear composed, but it's hard to stay calm. Keep these important skills in mind:

Recognize and acknowledge the fact that you're angry. Remember that anger is a normal, human emotion, and that it's okay to feel angry. In fact, it's healthy to express anger without being aggressive.

Make sure that you haven't misunderstood what the other person has done. If you're sure that the source of your anger was intentional, think about it for a while and try to figure out why it made you so angry. Talk about it with an uninvolved person, and decide whether you really need to confront the person with whom you're angry. Sometimes small annoyances dissipate. Sometimes, however, they escalate in your mind, and that's when you probably need to express your anger.

When appropriate, express your anger directly and specifically. Pick a good time and tell the person why you are angry. Be succinct and to the point, focusing on the specific behavior that triggered your anger. Keep your voice firm but not confrontational, and make direct eye contact. Don't attack or blame the person. Try not to say anything you'll regret later.

Avoid "black and white" thinking, and use "I" statements. Instead of saying things like "You never___," say "I'd prefer that you'd___, because then I'd feel___," or "I feel angry when you ___." This puts the focus on your feelings instead of blaming or confronting the other person. When you use "I" statements, you are empowering yourself.

Aim your expression of anger toward negotiation. When you express your anger, you are naturally deepening your relationship with the person with whom you are angry. Hopefully, when the situation is resolved, your relationship will be better, stronger, and more positive.

Everyone gets angry. When you're really angry, it's sometimes hard to control your actions. This anger is usually the result of trigger thoughts, internal emotions or reactions that spark and heighten your anger. They are natural and normal reactions, but they only serve to make you angrier. If you can learn to recognize them, you may be better able to control your anger in the future. Here are some examples of trigger thoughts:

I want it, and I'm entitled to it. When you feel that you are entitled to something, you feel that you deserve it. When you don't get what you want, you become angry. You can combat this by thinking:
- I can want something, but the other person can say no.
- Just as the other person has the right to say no, so do I.
- My desire doesn't obligate the other person to grant what I want.

If I scratch your back, you have to scratch mine. Do you ever feel that your actions obligate others to respond in a certain way? For example, if you clean your room, does it seem only fair that your mom should let you go to the movies? And if she doesn't let you go, does it seem unfair, even if her reasons are legitimate? Life isn't always "tit-for-tat." Keep these thoughts in mind:
- Her needs are just as important as mine.
- If each need is legitimate, then we can negotiate.

It's all black and white to me. If you're angry with someone, you sometimes justify your anger by deciding that everything he does is wrong. Conversely, if you're happy with him, he can do no wrong. If you're in a pattern of noticing only the bad in others, remember:
- Everyone does good things and bad things.
- Putting people into categories decreases the possibility of seeing the good things in them.

You're doing this just to make me angry. Sometimes we assume that we know why people do things that hurt us, but the truth is that often we don't know the motives behind their actions. For example, there's probably a good reason why your dad couldn't come to your game, but you're so angry that you decide it's because he doesn't care about you. Remember:
- To assume nothing. Give the person the chance to explain.
- That trying to read minds will get you nowhere.

Why can't you be more ___? It is futile to get people to change just because what they have done angers you. Just as they don't usually do things just to make you angry, they also won't change just because you want them to. Keep this idea in mind:
- People only change when they are able and motivated to change, and only when they want to.

TRIGGER THOUGHTS

"You NEVER" and "You ALWAYS!" As in, "You NEVER make what I want for dinner!" and "You ALWAYS give him the bigger piece of cake!" Exaggerating blows things out of proportion. It's not really NEVER and ALWAYS, is it? Remember:
* To try to be accurate in your view of a situation.
* To let the facts speak for themselves.

If you ___, then you'd _____. If/then assumptions go like this: "If my mom really loved me, then she'd make what I wanted for dinner," or "If my dad cared about me, then he would have come to my band recital." Sometimes circumstances are unavoidable. Just because people disappoint you doesn't mean they don't care about you. Think about this:
* Everyone has legitimate needs of their own.
* You can't assume that a person does something for a specific reason.

ANGER PERSONALITIES

There are different kinds of anger personalities. Each personality has its own negative traits, and each makes it hard for others to coexist with its "owner." If you "own" one of the following personalities, first admit it, then use what you've learned to improve your outlook.

Terrible tempered. This person is chronically angry. Everything makes him mad! He walks around with a chip on his shoulder. He's irritable, finds fault with everything, and reacts negatively to many things.

Hip-shooter. This person is impulsive and volatile to the point of being explosive. He can't wait his turn, and has a fit if he has to. He's quick to display his anger, and he's quick to forget it (while others are still feeling its effects).

Counter-attacker. This person hides his hurt and underlying pain by blaming and criticizing others. Something is wrong with everything! He has difficulty accepting responsibility for his own behavior and feelings.

Victim. This person suppresses his anger. He denies feeling angry while he's boiling mad underneath. He is sometimes called passive-aggressive. He expresses his anger in indirect ways, such as missing appointments, "accidentally" breaking someone else's favorite things or "unintentionally" hurting someone's feelings, and being accident-prone (so that others have to help him).

Nagger. This person never focuses on the issue or problem that's associated with his anger. He expresses his anger by complaining, which clouds the real issues. He loves to make mountains out of molehills.

Misinterpreter. This person never really listens. He makes conclusions about things without hearing the other side first. Consequently, his conclusions and decisions reflect what he's imagined, and he blows things out of proportion.

DEFUSING ANGER

The best way to defuse anger is to express it immediately, but that's not always possible. So sometimes it's better to find alternate ways of unloading angry feelings than confronting someone in the heat of the moment. Here are some alternatives:

Physical exercise. Exercise releases chemicals in your brain that make you feel better, even when you're angry. Vigorous exercise, like jogging, swimming, tennis, or basketball, provides physical release of pent-up energy. After a workout, the anger may not seem as strong or as important.

Physical expression. It's amazing how good it can feel to express your emotions in a physical way. This should be done in a private place so that no one can hear or distract you. Shouting, swearing, hitting a pillow, or punching a bag provides a physical release of tension and anger.

Expressing your anger to a third party. Talking about your anger to someone who can empathize and understand how you are feeling can be especially cathartic. He or she can give you words of support, offer you alternate ways of looking at the situation, or just lend a concerned ear while you blow off steam. Another effective anger-defuser is to write your feelings in a letter to the person who is making you angry. Wait until the next day, and, if you still feel angry, reread the letter, and decide whether sending it will really help the situation.

Psychological detachment. Sometimes the source of your anger can't be altered or changed. Your teacher won't give you a higher grade—period. That kid who's trying hard to be your friend isn't that bad. Your sister didn't lose your earring on purpose. You can resolve the situation in your mind, or you can resign yourself to it. If you think of alternate ways to view the situation and forget about getting even, you'll be on your way to anger resolution.

Relaxation. Relaxation is a gift you give yourself. If you know how to relax, you'll be able to do so when your anger is triggered. There are several tried-and-true relaxation techniques, including deep breathing, visualizing a calm and comforting scene, meditating, and listening to soothing music.

We often get angry with ourselves. This is a natural reaction when something doesn't go right, or we do something wrong. The feeling usually passes, but when it doesn't, it can escalate into a pattern of negative thinking.

Anger can be directed toward ourselves in the form of:
- Self-doubt: "I can't do this. No way."
- Low self-esteem: "I don't deserve it."
- Believing negative things: "I'm so fat. How can anyone like me?"
- Guilt about being angry: "Now she'll never speak to me again."
- Fear of someone else's anger at you: "I don't want to go with her, but she'll hate me if I say no."
- Putting blame on yourself: "He didn't do anything wrong. It was totally my fault. Why am I such a loser?"
- Feeling responsible for another's behavior: "If I'd cleaned my room, Mom would have bought me that sweater."
- Being a perfectionist: "If I don't get an 'A,' my teacher will hate me."
- Feeling helpless to change something: "What's the difference if I try to be nice? She won't like me anyway."

Anger can be used as protection or as an excuse to:
- Avoid confrontation: "If I tell her how I feel, she'll be angry."
- Avoid your own issues: "What if I work harder and my grades still don't get better?"
- Hurt yourself before others hurt you: "I might as well make a fool of myself. Everyone's going to laugh at me anyway."
- Feel safe or less of a threat to others: "I don't want to spoil their party so I won't go."
- Avoid responsibility for your own behavior: "He needs to be taught a lesson. I'll show him!"

Anger can be used in a positive way to:
- Change our expectations of ourselves: "This could be a rough situation, but I know I can handle it."
- Change our expectations of others: "She's really cool. Maybe she does like me after all!"
- Change to behavior that shows better self-esteem: "I don't have to prove myself. They'll like me for who I am."

DEALING WITH ANOTHER PERSON'S ANGER

Sometimes it's hard to know how to react when someone is angry with you. Here are some suggestions:

Just as you have the right to feel angry, so do others. Remember that anger is a secondary emotion that needs to be expressed. There's a difference between anger and aggression, which is an attempt to hurt someone or destroy something and an infringement on the rights of another person. It's better to know that the person is angry with you and to deal with it than to let it fester.

Just because someone's angry at you doesn't mean you should feel angry with him. You have to control your own feelings as you listen to what he's saying. "Losing it" will only make things worse.

If a person is aggressive toward you, remember that it is because he is feeling weak and helpless. The other person is probably so mad that he doesn't know what else to do. This is your chance to help him back off, calm down, and talk it out. If this isn't possible, seek the help of someone who's qualified to handle the situation.

Focus attention on the task to be completed and not the person's anger. If you're having a quarrel about something that you and the other person must do together, don't get sidetracked or derailed by the argument. Try to stay focused on what needs to be done, and keep trying to get him involved.

Use self-talk. You can tell yourself things like "I'm good at handling other people's anger" and "His anger is really annoying, but it's his problem, not mine." Deep breathing can help, too.

Warm words can do wonders. Just when he least expects it, try complimenting the other person or saying something really nice to him. This can help him regain control.

Congratulate yourself on handling the situation rationally and with control. It's not easy to deal with someone who's being really difficult. If you can handle it yourself and help the other person through it, you'll be prepared for the next situation.

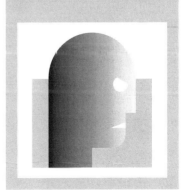

Sometimes we hide our anger from ourselves, but sooner or later it surfaces. The longer and harder we try to suppress it, the more difficult it may be to deal with when it does come out. People who say that they never get angry are fooling themselves—if they feel annoyed, frustrated, irritable, or upset, it's a sure bet that there's anger in there too. And if it's in there, it has to come out eventually.

The trick is to recognize and express your anger before it overpowers you. Here's a list of things that can help you determine whether you are recognizing your anger. If you check more than four, you may be suppressing hidden anger.

☐ Not getting things done (homework, chores, etc.)

☐ Always being late

☐ Sarcasm in conversation or lack of seriousness

☐ Being overpolite, constantly cheerful, or adopting a "grin-and-bear-it" attitude

☐ Smiling when you're hurting inside

☐ Difficulty falling asleep

☐ Nightmares or night sweats

☐ Boredom, loss of interest in things you used to enjoy

☐ Excessive tiredness

☐ Becoming very angry at seemingly insignificant injustices

☐ Sleeping more than usual

☐ Waking up feeling tired rather than rested

☐ Clenched jaws, especially when sleeping

☐ Facial or foot movements, fist clenching, or other repeated physical acts done unintentionally or of which you are unaware

☐ Stiff or sore neck and/or shoulder muscles

☐ Periods of feeling down for no reason

ACTIVITY: I WAS SO ANGRY WHEN . . .

Think about a recent time when you felt really angry and then answer these questions. This exercise may help you deal with your anger in a more constructive manner in the future.

What happened that made you feel so angry? _____

I was angry because:
- ☐ I was let down
- ☐ my feelings were hurt
- ☐ I was rejected
- ☐ I was misunderstood
- ☐ I didn't meet my own expectations
- ☐ someone didn't live up to my expectations
- ☐ other: _____

On a scale from 1 (mildly angry) to 5 (furious), I felt _____

What was said that led to your feelings of anger? _____

What did <u>you</u> say that might have contributed to the anger?
_____

I was physically aware of my anger because I felt or experienced:
- ☐ shortness of breath
- ☐ overheated
- ☐ stomachache
- ☐ headache
- ☐ tense
- ☐ dizzy
- ☐ other: _____

Here's what went through my mind: _____

As a result of the anger, I also felt:
- ☐ helpless
- ☐ fear
- ☐ anxious
- ☐ misunderstood
- ☐ sad
- ☐ rejected
- ☐ hurt
- ☐ other: _____

I dealt with my anger by:
- ☐ becoming quiet
- ☐ withdrawing
- ☐ yelling/screaming
- ☐ crying
- ☐ talking about it
- ☐ being physically aggressive
- ☐ hurt
- ☐ other: _____

I felt ___ satisfied ___ unsatisfied with the situation.
Here's why: _____

CONFLICT RESOLUTION

Conflict Resolution

Conflict resolution is a necessary component of any successful academic program. This chapter defines the term "conflict" and integrates a variety of problem-solving techniques that include respecting the feelings of others, the art of negotiation, peer mediation, and cooperation versus competition. The activity pages offer handouts focused on awareness of feelings and practicing negotiation.

Time Allotment

Two 50-minute sessions integrated into a series of 50-minute class periods.

Goal

To identify alternative methods of coping with conflicts and develop increased communication and better relationships.

Objectives

- A student will understand the definition of "conflict."
- A student will learn to recognize the importance of respecting another person's feelings.
- A student will become familiar with five skills needed to negotiate conflicts.
- A student will be able to identify seven elements of conflict resolution.
- A student will be able to practice the five steps needed to help resolve a conflict.

WHAT IS CONFLICT?

Conflict is a part of everyone's daily life. Without it, our world would be pretty bleak and unexciting: There would be no growth, no challenge, no change. Differences of opinion may create conflict, but they also stimulate creative thinking and move people to think harder, work toward goals, and stand up for what they believe. In fact, studies have shown that kids from families that encourage dissension and disagreement have higher self-esteem than those from families that discourage open expression of negative feelings.

Traditionally, conflict has got a bad rap. When kids are asked what comes to mind when they hear the word "conflict," many say "anger," "hostility," "argument," "violence," "hate," or "aggression." We learn to approach conflict with a negative attitude, because it can cause pain, stress, fear, and problems with relationships. We usually respond to it aggressively (violently), seek the help of an authority figure, or ignore it completely (and deny our angry feelings). But the better way is to work to resolve the conflict.

It's important to recognize the difference between conflict and violence. Conflicts and disagreements can be healthy. Violence is never good. Conflicts can foster understanding, while violence usually causes more misunderstanding and hurt. When conflicts are resolved peacefully, rather than through physical force or verbal put-downs, everyone wins. Conflict resolution:

- Heals hurt feelings
- Gives people control over their feelings
- Fosters assertiveness
- Builds trust and honesty
- Fosters intimacy
- Encourages personal growth and identity
- Helps people take responsibility for their feelings and actions
- Keeps communication open
- Gives people the courage to disagree

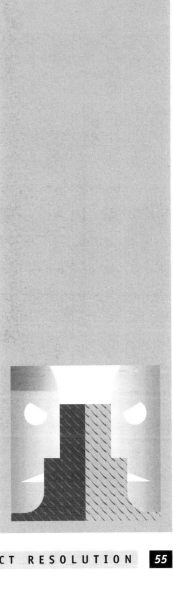

Because conflicts in schools have become so common, conflict resolution experts have suggested that "Resolution" be the fourth "R" in our educational system, along with "Reading," "'Riting," and "'Rithmetic." While conflict is inevitable, it can have both negative and positive effects. It can result in violence or even death, but it can also help people gain new perspectives. It's a sure bet that, sooner or later, you're going to have a conflict with a classmate, friend, or teacher. Keep the following conflict resolution elements in mind:

• **Be aware of what makes you very angry.** Learn the difference between healthy and unhealthy ways of expressing anger, and learn how to channel your anger nonviolently. Realize that even if you "win" an argument through violence, the other person will probably try to get even, resulting in another conflict.

• **Face the conflict rather than avoid it.** The idea of dealing with a problem is often worse than actually doing it. Think about what you do to avoid conflict. Do you deny that anything's wrong? Do you become overly nice so the other person won't be mad at you? Do you put off confrontation?

• **Respect yourself and your interests, and respect the other person and his interests.** Your interests should always come first, as long as no one is hurt in the process. You should feel secure that what you want is important. Don't allow yourself to be bullied into thinking otherwise.

• **Respect the reality of cultural difference.** Not everyone does things the way you do. Use differences as learning opportunities.

• **Know the difference between an "interest" and a "position."** Your interest isn't something that can be negotiated, while your position is. When conflicting parties tell each other about their interests, it's easier to find a solution that's agreeable to both of them. What's more, they may find that they have mutual interests.

• **Listen carefully and make sure you're understood.** When people feel that they are understood, they are more willing to resolve conflicts. If you listen so that the other person really feels understood, you'll find that the other person will listen to you in the same way.

• **If a person refuses to negotiate, realize that you don't have to stay in the relationship.** If someone will only cooperate on his terms, you usually have the choice to walk away.

The idea of dealing with a problem is often worse than actually doing it.

When conflicting parties tell each other about their interests, it's easier to find a solution that's agreeable to both of them.

RESPECTING THE FEELINGS OF OTHERS

Conflicts are born from conflicting feelings. One person feels one way, and the other disagrees. Does this mean that one is right and the other is wrong? Maybe, but not necessarily. No one has the power or the right to tell another person that she shouldn't feel a certain way, or that she shouldn't have a particular opinion. When you really think about it, feelings are among the only things that are truly "yours"—others may do things to make you feel a certain way, but ultimately your feelings are yours and yours alone.

It's important to learn to understand another's perspective. Here are some of the basic elements of perspective-taking as it relates to conflict resolution:

• Everyone has a unique perspective, a different way of viewing the world. It's safe to say that no two people see the same situation or understand the same message in exactly the same way.

• When attempting to resolve a conflict, you have to be able to take the other person's perspective and try to envision how the conflict looks to her. She needs to do the same for you.

• Your perspective on a given subject can change, and you can have different perspectives at different times.

The more you're able to see the other person's perspective, the better you'll be able to understand the issue.

• The more you're able to see the other person's perspective, the better you'll be able to understand the issue. This is called empathizing, or understanding another person's feelings so well that you almost know how she feels.

• When you're an empathetic person, you are able to understand how passionately the other person feels about something, even if you don't agree with her. You may even be able to "feel" her pain, anger, or hurt, but you will be able to remain neutral to it.

• It helps to do a "perception check" to be sure that you understand how the other person really feels. To do this, you

1. describe what you think the other person is feeling,

2. ask whether your perception is right, and

3. accept the person's feelings without disapproval or judgment.

THE ELEMENTS OF "WIN-WIN"

When you're in a conflict, winning means that you get what you want in that situation. Most people think that one person has to win and the other has to lose. Consequently, both people try as hard as they can to win, and things can get pretty difficult. When they're thinking only of themselves, it's hard to reach a solution to the problem. Approaching a conflict as if both parties can win takes the attention away from the individuals and focuses on solving the problem. If the individuals decide to work together, they can try to achieve mutual satisfaction, creating a win-win situation in which neither person loses.

Here's a hypothetical situation. Andy's missed class several times because he attended meetings for an activity. He tells the teacher he needs more time to study for the math test, but his teacher, Ms. Bartlett, won't let him have the extra time because she feels it would be unfair to the other kids. Both have good reasons for their positions. But the situation should be viewed as one in which both Andy and Ms. Bartlett want the best possible outcome. In other words, Andy wants to do well on the test, and Ms. Bartlett wants him to do well, but if she gives in to him, the other students may see this as being unfair. Who should give in?

If Ms. Bartlett says no, you could say that she has "won" and Andy has "lost." If Andy gets his extra time to study, does this mean that Ms. Bartlett "loses" and Andy "wins?" Wouldn't it be better for both parties to discuss the options? Possibly Andy could take the test a day later, and Ms. Bartlett could allow him to do this in the interest of learning.

In this situation, Andy and Ms. Bartlett become two equal parties with their own needs instead of student and teacher. This is a tricky situation because it blurs the boundaries of the student-teacher relationship, but it can be resolved if both of them focus on the importance of the outcome. In the interest of win-win, they should:

• **Define the problem.** Instead of focusing on the reasons for the problem, the parties should discuss their different points of view and the potential positive outcome of the situation.

• **Find a solution.** Brainstorming, or coming up with a range of ideas for solving the problem, is the next step. Once possible solutions are identified, the best one is chosen by both parties.

• **Put the win-win solution into practice.** This is where the task is performed as planned.

• **Reflect on how the solution worked and build on it.** The parties talk about how well the plan worked (or didn't work), how they feel about it, whether they should change anything about it for the future, and whether they should try something new next time.

Approaching a conflict as if both parties can win takes the attention away from the individuals and focuses on solving the problem.

Instead of focusing on the reasons for the problem, the parties should discuss their different points of view and the potential positive outcome of the situation.

THE ART OF NEGOTIATION

Negotiating is a way of getting what you want from others. It is a back-and-forth kind of communication designed to end in agreement. It involves a peaceful resolution of a conflict, without aggression or violence.

Many people don't know how to negotiate. Instead, they state what they want, and when they don't get it, they feel frustrated. They either give up or try to achieve their needs through force. But it's important to know the skills of negotiation, because they will help you get what you want and need through your school years and beyond. These skills include:

• **Defining the conflict.** Both parties express what they want and how they feel about the conflict. They can also talk about what caused the conflict and exactly what happened. They listen with empathy and respect, suspend judgment, and resolve to cooperate.

• **Defining the reasons for the conflict.** Both parties explain the rationale underlying their position in the conflict. Then each paraphrases what the other has said to make sure that there is mutual understanding.

• **Understanding each other's perspective.** Perspective-taking helps each party acknowledge the other's thinking, but it doesn't mean that they have to agree.

• **Formulating solutions.** It's best to come up with two or three plans and evaluate the logistics of each.

• **Coming to an agreement.** The parties pick the best solution together. Even if it's a compromise, remember that everyone will benefit from it.

It's also important to remember that not every issue is negotiable. There's a difference between a negotiable issue (it's okay to wait until tomorrow to do your homework when it's not due till the end of the week) and a non-negotiable one (you have to do your homework if it's due tomorrow). If someone tries to negotiate with you on a non-negotiable issue (your friend wants you to take drugs and you don't want to), you should always say no.

It's also important to remember that not every issue is negotiable.

Mediation is a process in which a neutral third party, or someone who is not involved in a particular conflict, helps people resolve their differences. Mediation is a peaceful, planned process, facilitated by a mediator who has been trained in mediation skills.

Peer mediation has become popular in schools because it gives students the chance to work out their differences without the involvement of teachers or other authority figures. Peer mediators are students who have been trained to help other students listen to each other and work things out together. They are usually students who are well-liked, but they're not necessarily the most popular. Students like this arrangement because it's easier to talk to people their own age, and they feel that a peer mediator knows how they feel better than a staff member.

Peer mediation has become popular in schools because it gives students the chance to work out their differences without the involvement of teachers or other authority figures.

Peer mediators are impartial, empathetic, and respectful to those who are in dispute. They remain neutral, fair, and unbiased, and they're good listeners. They always keep things confidential. Schools have reported that peer mediation has played a large part in decreases in hostility and tension between students. The ultimate goal is for students to learn to work things out on their own.

Mediators must follow a set of steps in order to help resolve a conflict. These include:

• **Introduction.** The mediator introduces himself as mediator and explains his function. He then asks if both parties want his help in solving the problem. If they agree, a quiet place is found, and the mediator gets the parties to agree on (1) trying to work out a resolution to the problem, (2) listening to the other person until he is finished talking, (3) no put-downs or name-calling, and (4) confidentiality.

• **Listening and reflecting.** The mediator asks the first person to tell what happened, and then paraphrases what was said. The first person is asked to tell how he felt, and the mediator paraphrases these words as well. The process repeats itself with the second person.

• **Brainstorming solutions.** Both parties are asked by the mediator to talk about what they could have done differently, and what they can do now to solve the problem. Both parties take turns speaking, and the mediator paraphrases what is said.

• **Deciding on solutions.** The mediator helps the parties find a solution that is mutually agreeable. When one is found, the mediator repeats the solution and asks each person if he agrees with what's been decided. If both agree, the mediation process is finished.

UNDERSTANDING PREJUDICE AND INTOLERANCE

Conflict often arises between people from different cultures, races, or religions. Although the conflict can be the result of a specific argument or fight, it can also occur just because of these differences. Prejudice can be hard to resist, especially if your parents and/or your friends feel it and communicate it to you. But it's a negative feeling, and it breeds more hatred and contempt. In the end, it gets you nowhere.

The more you get to know people, the more you find to like about them. This includes people who are different from you. If you feel threatened or frightened when you are with such people, or if you discriminate against them, there are some concrete ways to change your attitude:

• Think about who you consider to be part of your group, and then think about it in a different way. You may be of Italian descent, or Jewish, or African American. The people who are from your culture are certainly part of your "group." But think about other groups to which you belong. There are probably kids from a lot of different cultures and races in your class at school. You're all part of the same group. If you belong to a club, the same is probably true. When you enter a chat room on the Internet you become part of another kind of group. You don't even know the people you're talking to, or what their culture is, or their religion, or race. And it doesn't really matter, does it?

• Think about the similarities you have with other people in your world. The people you feel prejudiced toward may have very different habits and lifestyles, but it's likely that their values, or the things they consider important, are pretty similar to yours. The only way to find out is to get to know someone who's different from you.

• Think about how differences can be a positive thing. We can react to difference with fear and contempt, or we can view it with interest and respect. It's been proven that the more kinds of abilities and traits a group of people can call upon to solve its problems, the more likely it is that a solution will be found. The idea isn't to give up your individuality; it's to recognize that your way is not the only way, and it's not necessarily the best way.

• Think about how all people are dependent on each other. In 1776, Benjamin Franklin warned the Continental Congress, "We must, indeed, all hang together, or most assuredly we shall all hang separately." By this he meant that the 13 original colonies had to put aside their differences and work toward their common goal of becoming one nation.

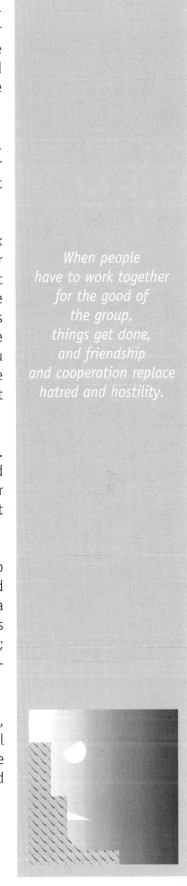

When people have to work together for the good of the group, things get done, and friendship and cooperation replace hatred and hostility.

As young children, we are taught to cooperate with others. Why is cooperation always better than conflict? Because more often than not, the cooperative solution benefits everyone. It fosters kindness, which is something that makes everyone feel good, no matter how young or old.

Cooperation doesn't always mean that you have to do what you're told. It can also mean working together toward a mutual goal. To cooperate with someone, you don't have to be together or even in the same place—think of all of the situations in which two or three or ten or hundreds of people cooperate to make something happen.

Competition, on the other hand, breeds conflict. In schools and in social situations, there's a lot of competition—for grades, for performance in sports, for the coolest clothes, and so on. Competition is so much a part of our lives that it's hard to imagine life without it. If cooperation were as much a part of life, there'd be less conflict, and there would probably be no need for this chapter.

Some people think that competition builds confidence and self-esteem. But this isn't really true—competition only boosts self-esteem if you win, and winning, as we're told, isn't everything. When you win, someone else loses.

Others feel that cooperation allows lazy people to get a free ride on the backs of hard workers. This isn't true either, because when kids cooperate, everyone takes part in getting the work done. If they don't, it's a sure bet that the other kids will let them know that their laziness is unacceptable. Cooperation requires everyone to contribute, and when this happens, many different opinions, knowledge levels, and skills come into play.

Of course, competition is necessary sometimes. If we don't learn to compete, we fall behind. Competition isn't a bad thing until it begins to hurt others. Cooperation is better, however, because it often leads to a greater good than competition, and it always ends up in a win-win situation.

ACTIVITY: HOW WOULD YOU FEEL, WHAT WOULD YOU DO?

Different people have different reactions to different conflicts. Some are really bothered when they have a fight with someone, and others are able to let things slide. On the lines below, write about how you'd feel if the situation happened to you, and how you'd resolve the conflict. Then, discuss them with a partner to see if you agree or disagree.

Your lunch buddy tells you not to sit at her table anymore.

A classmate tells a lie about you.

Someone butts in front of you and gets the last ticket to the concert.

Your teacher tells you she can't change your grade.

Your mother accuses you of something you didn't do.

You and your best friend both like the same boy/girl.

You want to go to the movies and your friend wants to stay home.

ACTIVITY: PRACTICING NEGOTIATION

Here's a way to practice negotiation with a partner. Think of a conflict that you have with your partner (or make one up), and then practice the steps of negotiation.

The problem/conflict is _____

_____ .

Step 1: Agree to negotiate.
Say out loud, "I agree to listen to you and take turns talking, and I agree to cooperate to solve the conflict."

Step 2: Hear the differing points of view.
Using "I" statements, Student A tells his view of the problem by telling what he did: "I was _____;"
why he did it: "I did it because _____;"
how he felt when he was doing it: "I felt _____;"and how he feels about it now: "I feel _____."

Student B then clarifies Student A's view of the problem, and adds his point of view. The process then reverses itself with Student B telling his view, and Student A clarifying it.

Step 3: Tell what you want to happen.
Again, using an "I" statement, Student A says, "I want_____
because _____."
Student B does the same. Both discuss what would happen if the problem isn't solved, and both answer the question, "If you were me, what would you think?"

Step 4: Create win-win options.
Together, the students brainstorm at least three solutions to the problem. Anything that comes to mind is okay, and neither judges the other's ideas.

Step 5: Think about the options.
The students discuss the plausibility of each option in formulating a solution.

Step 6: Resolve the conflict.
They come up with a "who/what/where/when/how" plan of action. Then the students summarize what they've agreed to do, by saying, "I have agreed to _____."

VIOLENCE AWARENESS

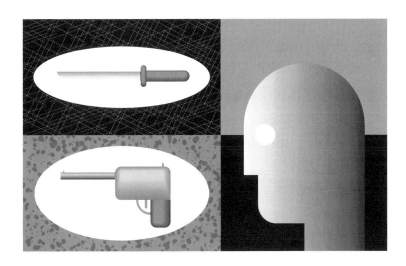

Violence Awareness

This chapter focuses on outlining facts about violence, the characteristics found in violent children, factors that contribute to violent behavior, dating violence, gun safety, and ways to avoid and deal with violent behavior. Two handouts are included: one that focuses on raising awareness of what to do in a violent situation, and a violence questionnaire.

Time Allotment

Two 50-minute sessions integrated into a series of 50-minute class periods.

Goal

To provide information and statistics on violence and violent behavior in order to help raise awareness and prevent conflicts and tragedies.

Objectives

- A student will become aware of at least six statistics on violence.
- A student will be able to recognize at least ten characteristics of someone who may have violent tendencies.
- A student will become familiar with the basics of gun safety.
- A student will be able to identify six factors that influence people to act violently.
- A student will be able to verbalize at least six out of ten suggestions for avoiding violence.

SCHOOL VIOLENCE

Recent events have shown that children and teens are increasingly in danger of being victims of violence. If you are angry about having to worry about violence at school, you have every right to your feelings. Nothing is scarier than thinking that you could be a victim of a shooting, bombing, or other act of violence. Much research is being done on why violence has become such a menacing problem at school. Here are some observations:

• **Violence is not just a city problem.** The amount of violence in suburban school districts is only about one-third lower than that in urban settings.

• **Most injuries from violence occur between people who know each other.** It used to be thought that only gang members got into fights, but most arguments that get out of control and end up in fights occur between schoolmates and acquaintances.

• **Many kids deny it, but TV violence is a factor.** From the time you were little, you have watched cartoons and other TV shows that sent the message, "If you are smart, you will use violence instead of reason to get what you want from other people."

• **Although school districts have forbidden them, some kids still carry guns.** Kids who have been taught that fighting is the best way to handle conflict think nothing of pulling out a gun and using it. If it seems like the right thing to do, they'll do it.

• **What schools can do to prevent violence.** Today's schools need to be prepared for any type of incident that may occur. Schools must increase their collaborative efforts involving students, parents, and outside agencies. Susan Gorin, Executive Director of the National Association of School Psychologists (NASP), outlines a number of recommendations for schools to consider as proactive initiatives to prevent violence. Ms Gorin suggests schools should:
• Increase involvement of parents and the community in schools
• Improve school climate
• Develop an early identification system
• Prepare resources to serve identified students in the school and community
• Create a system that permits the confidential communication of known or suspected threats to trained school personnel
• Adopt peer mediation and peer intervention programs
• Create a system in the schools that connects students to adults

It is your responsibility to learn how to resolve conflict constructively, without the use of force and violence.

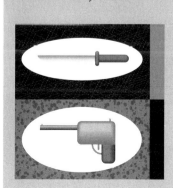

(continued)

(continued)

Within this book, there is a wealth of advice on handling anger constructively, keeping calm, and communicating with people who are provoking you to fight. It takes a lot of courage not to get into a fight—to walk away from someone who is ready to "teach you a lesson."

It is your responsibility to learn how to resolve conflict constructively, without the use of force and violence. In a violent resolution of a conflict, someone always wins and the other person always loses. In a non-violent resolution, both parties win.

THE CHARACTERISTICS OF VIOLENT KIDS

While it is mostly the responsibility of school officials to identify kids who may be violent, it's up to you, too, to know the characteristics. Violent kids are often bullies and they demonstrate—or talk to others about—feelings of isolation, anger, depression, and frustration. If you're concerned about school violence, you should know the risk factors. If you think a classmate (or anyone you encounter) may have violent tendencies, it's imperative that you tell an adult immediately.

The National School Safety Center offers this checklist as a starting point. The violent child:

- Has a history of tantrums and uncontrollable angry outbursts.
- Resorts to name calling, cursing, or abusive language when challenged.
- Makes violent threats when angry.
- Has previously brought a weapon to school.
- Has a background of serious disciplinary problems at school and in the community.
- Has a background of drug, alcohol, or other substance abuse or dependency.
- Is on the fringe of his/her peer group with few or no close friends.
- Is preoccupied with weapons, explosives, or similar devices.
- Has been truant, suspended, or expelled from school.
- Is cruel to animals.
- Has little or no supervision and support from parents or caring adults.
- Has witnessed or been a victim of abuse or neglect in the home.
- Has been bullied and/or bullies peers or younger children.
- Blames others for his/her difficulties and problems.
- Prefers TV shows, movies, and/or music with violent themes.
- Prefers reading books and other materials with violent themes, rituals, and/or abuse.
- Writes about anger and the dark side of life in school essays and writing projects.
- Is involved with a gang or antisocial group "on the fringe."
- Has talked about or attempted suicide.

The violent child is often depressed and/or has significant mood swings.

Homicide is the second-leading cause of death for people 15 to 24 years of age. It is the leading cause of death for African American and Hispanic youth in this age group. In 1996, more than 6,500 people in this age group were homicide victims, an average of 18 youth homicide victims a day in the United States. That's the equivalent of more than 12 large commercial airline plane crashes in which there were no survivors in a single year. Other statistics include:

- Between July 1, 1994, and June 30, 1998, there were 173 school violence incidents in the United States.

- In 1997, 14 American children were killed with guns each day.

- In 1996, 85 percent of homicide victims aged 15 to 19 were killed with a firearm.

- Murders of juveniles between ages 12 and 17 increased 95 percent between 1980 and 1994.

- Teenagers are two-and-a-half times more likely than adults to be victims of violence.

- More than 75 percent of the homicides of teenagers involve people who know each other. In 1995, 22 percent of youth murder victims were murdered by family members, 37 percent by acquaintances, and 13 percent by strangers.

- The perpetrator and victim are of the same race about 90 percent of the time.

- For each violent death, there are an estimated 100-plus nonfatal injuries caused by violence.

- In one survey, 47 percent of students in grades 7 through 12 said it was "easy" for them to get a gun.

- In his lifetime, a typical 11-year-old has seen 100,000 acts of violence on TV, including 8,000 murders.

- In a poll of 2,000 teenagers from urban and suburban areas, one in eight youths said they carry a weapon for protection. In high-violence neighborhoods, this statistic increased to two in five.

WHAT MAKES KIDS VIOLENT?

It's not always easy to predict that someone will have a violent reaction to a situation. That's one of the things that's so scary about violence—it lashes out at you when you least expect it, because most of us expect others to be kind, caring, and just. Sometimes, however, people lose control when certain factors come into play.

• **Kids use violence to express themselves or their anger.** Sometimes they can't see any other way to get their point across. Of course, if they'd calm down and think of better ways to communicate, they wouldn't be violent in the first place.

• **Kids use violence to get what they want.** It's a handy tool when you want to control others, or hurt people who have hurt you. Initially, violence may get you what you want, but sooner or later it will turn against you.

• **Kids are violent because they witness violence at home.** Have you heard the expression "Children model what they see?" In the violence context, it's a good bet that if parents are violent, their children will also have violent tendencies, unless they get help. If they watch a lot of TV, they may get the message that violence is an acceptable means of getting their way.

• **Kids are violent because of peer pressure.** Gang members are the best example of this. They have to be violent and intimidating to others to remain in their peer group. They think that they will gain the respect of others if they make people fear them through violence.

• **Kids are violent because they have access to guns.** This is a no-brainer: If parents are negligent enough to leave guns around the house, sooner or later a child will get the message that it's okay to use them.

• **Kids are violent because they feel rejected and socially isolated.** Most of these children are extremely aggressive as young children, and when they don't get the help and support they need, they progress to more severe aggression or violence.

Initially, violence may get you what you want, but sooner or later it will turn against you.

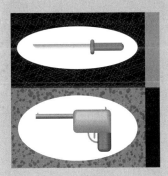

DATING VIOLENCE

Dating, love, and sex should never be about violence. They are meant to be pleasant and fulfilling experiences with no room for force and coercion. Unfortunately, however, many teens are reluctant to say "no" to something they don't want to do in case their dates will feel rejected. Many individuals use force to get what they want, even though the outcome only brings rejection and unhappiness.

Jealousy is a common source of violence, for both sexes. But someone who loves you should never kick, slap, or hit you. And if someone really cares about you, there's no need for him/her to check up on you and your activities.

If you think you can hold onto someone through sex, think again. Love and trust are what's important. If you're not interested in being sexually involved, someone who really loves you will understand this, and will never try to break down your resistance by force or otherwise.

Dating violence can take the form of sexual assault, physical violence, and verbal or emotional abuse. Date rape includes forced sexual intercourse, sexual abuse without penetration, attempted rape, or sexual intimidation.

Teens who are most at risk for dating violence are those who drink on dates and/or abuse drugs. If you think you're at risk, keep these points in mind:

• **Don't get drunk.** This way, you're less likely to be in a vulnerable position and you'll know when and how to say "no." And don't be fooled that things will be fine because you know the person: victims of sexual violence usually know the perpetrator well.

• **Avoid trouble.** If you're a high school student, you should probably avoid parties where there's a lot of alcohol and a lot of potential for trouble.

• **Say "no" and mean it.** Let the people you date know that when you say "no," you mean "not now, not ever." If you change your mind later, that's a different story.

If you're a victim of date rape, you should have a medical exam that includes tests for sexually transmitted diseases, a "morning after" pill (for girls), and crisis counseling. Never feel embarrassed about talking with friends and others who can help. And never let people try to convince you that it was your fault.

Teens who are most at risk for dating violence are those who drink on dates and/or abuse drugs.

GUN SAFETY

Like it or not, guns are part of our culture. People buy them for hunting, for personal protection, or as a hobby. You may have them in your home, or you may know someone who has one. Either way, you should know the basics of gun safety:

1. Always assume that a gun is loaded and ready to fire. Even if you've handled a gun in the past, you should never touch one without adult supervision. You may think it's not loaded when it really is.

2. Never point a gun at anyone. Never assume it's safe to pull the trigger, even if you think there's no bullet in the barrel that's to be fired.

3. Guns should be stored properly. This means unloaded in a locked place, with the ammunition also in a locked place.

4. Recognize a gun at risk. If your parents keep a gun in the house for safety purposes, it's most likely kept in a place that is easily accessible. This greatly increases the risks of unsafe gun use. If people become emotionally upset or depressed, the likelihood of a gun accident is 100 percent greater if a gun is available.

5. If you see someone mishandling a weapon, call 911. This doesn't have to be a stranger—it can be a family member, a friend, or someone else you know.

6. Never touch a "fake" weapon. If you don't know if it's real, assume it is.

7. If a friend's family keeps a gun in an unsafe place, or uses it in an unsafe manner, tell someone. If the parents are negligent with the gun, do everything you can to avoid going to that friend's house and tell an adult about it.

8. Never take a gun to school. These days, there are strict rules about guns in school. Never take one, not even a fake one, and report anyone who does.

9. Don't let anyone who has a gun think they are impressing you. Having a gun is not cool — ever. If you see someone with one, walk away and then report it.

Having a gun is not cool — ever!

AVOIDING VIOLENCE

Look as if you know what you're doing and where you're going.

Unfortunately, the odds of your being a victim of violence are greater than ever. Instead of putting yourself in harm's way, remember to do the following:

• **Avoid dangerous situations.** Everyone knows it's dangerous to hitchhike, go places with strangers, and walk alone after dark. Although acts of violence against you aren't really your fault, doing such things makes you more vulnerable, and certainly less safe.

• **Avoid gangs and other groups of kids who hang out with nothing to do.** Having nothing to do turns into boredom very quickly, and acts of violence occur "for the fun of it."

• **Always walk on main streets, especially if you're alone.** This way you're visible to other people, and less likely to be abducted.

• **Don't do anything alone after dark.** In certain neighborhoods, even walking your dog alone is dangerous. If you have to drive somewhere, keep the car doors locked at all times.

• **Don't look like a victim.** Look as if you know what you're doing and where you're going. If you're walking alone, go directly to your destination. Stopping at public places where there are other people is okay.

• **If someone suddenly confronts or attacks you, yell "Fire!"** This will attract attention, and the perpetrator will most likely run away.

• **If you're attacked, fight back.** Hit the attacker's pressure points—put your fingers in his eyes or grab his throat.

• **If you think you're being followed, go to the closest place where there will be other people.** Go to a business or to the nearest house and knock on the door. The owners will most likely let you use the phone to call someone if you explain what's happening.

• **If you're followed while driving, drive to the nearest police station.** Never go home, even if you know someone is at your home.

• **If you know someone who's considering an act of violence, tell a person who can help.** You could save a life.

WHAT TO DO WHEN SOMEONE GETS VIOLENT

Sometimes it's hard to tell that a conflict is escalating until it's almost too late. Tempers flare and harsh words are spoken. All of a sudden, one of the parties really loses it. What should you do?

• **Understand what's in an angry person's mind.** People who are ready to fight are unhappy about many aspects of their lives—perhaps being neglected by parents or poor performance in school. This affects the way they act and think. Most of the time, if such a person picks a fight with you, he's taking his angry feelings out on you. Fighting may actually make him feel better, temporarily.

• **Don't make things worse.** There are certain things you should never do (and no other person should ever do to you). These include insulting, making fun of someone, or disrespecting him, putting down his family members, and cursing him out. Derogatory racial or ethnic comments are also a bad idea.

• **Don't get in the middle.** Keep calm. If the fight isn't directed at you, stay out of it and get help from an adult. If you are in the middle of it, try to resolve the conflict by talking it out, or, if the person is too upset or you feel afraid, simply walk away.

• **Review the situation.** Keep asking yourself "What is this fight about?" "Is it really about me?" "Am I afraid?" "Is it possible to talk this out?" "Should I get help now before it's too late?"

• **Speak to the "human" in the other person.** Even if you're being dumped on or insulted, remember that everyone has a good side. Ask him why he's so mad at you, and try to find out what you did that was so awful. If he thinks you did something offensive, tell him you didn't mean to do it (if you didn't), and apologize. Listen to what he has to say, and state your understanding of the problem. Say, "I have nothing against you. Is this worth fighting about?" If he stops to think about it, he may decide it's not.

Think about this: A wise observer once said, "The best way to defeat an enemy is to turn him into a friend."

Even if you're being dumped on or insulted, remember that everyone has a good side.

ACTIVITY: HOW WOULD YOU HANDLE IT?

For your personal safety, it's important to think about how you would handle a potentially violent situation before it actually happens. What would you do in the following situations? By now you probably know what you should do. For each answer, explain why you think it's the best solution.

1. You're walking down the street with a bunch of friends, and a group of kids comes toward you looking for a fight. Do you:

a. Try to avoid the fight?
b. Pick a fight with them before they do it to you?
c. See what happens and then decide?
Why? _____

2. Your friend wants to use his BB gun to shoot at squirrels from the second-floor window of his house. Do you:

a. Let him do it and watch?
b. Make him give you a few turns?
c. Tell him not to do it, and, if he doesn't listen, go home?
Why? _____

3. You're at a party where there's lots of drugs and alcohol. There aren't any parents or other adults around. Do you:

a. Call your parents to come to get you or find another way to get home?
b. Hang out and join in the fun?
c. Stay at the party and hope it doesn't get busted?
Why? _____

4. A kid you think is cute asks you to go for a drive. You don't know him very well, and you know he's from a rough crowd. Do you:

a. Go on the date alone?
b. Ask if you can bring a friend?
c. Tell him you want to get to know him better?
Why? _____

5. Your best friend gets into a fight over a racial slur. Do you:

a. Join in the fight to help your friend?
b. Try to get the fighting parties to stop and calm down?
c. Get an adult to break up the fight?
Why? _____

You're at a party where there's lots of drugs and alcohol. What do you do?

ACTIVITY: VIOLENCE QUESTIONNAIRE

As safe as you may think your school and community, there are dangers in every town and city in the United States. As a responsible citizen and student, you need to think about the following questions. Answer them honestly, and, if you don't know the answers, find out before it's too late.

- In your town, where can you hang out safely? _____

- Are there alcohol and drugs at the parties you go to? _____

- Do you think it's okay to be at such parties? _____
  Why or why not? _____

- What would you do if you felt unsafe at a party? _____

- What would you do if you felt unsafe on a town or city street? _____

- Do you think it's important for adults to be around when you're at a friend's house? _____
  Why or why not? _____

- Is it okay for people you hardly know to come over to your house when your parents aren't home? _____
  Why or why not? _____

- What would you do if someone showed you a gun or knife? _____

- Is it safe to walk alone in your neighborhood? _____
  Why or why not? _____

- Is it safe to hitchhike in your town or city? _____
  Why or why not? _____

- Do you feel safe at your school? _____
  Why or why not? _____

- Does your school have a violence prevention plan? _____
  If not, do you think it should? _____
  Why or why not? _____

Is it safe to hitchhike in your town or city?

COPING WITH DEPRESSION

Coping with Depression

This chapter offers information about depression, including its signs, symptoms, and causes. The chapter offers material that can help a child ascertain whether he is really depressed or just "down in the dumps." It offers realistic coping skills to decrease the symptoms of depression, and suggestions on dealing with a friend who may be depressed.

Time Allotment

Two 50-minute sessions integrated into a series of 50-minute class periods.

Goal

To provide information on and coping skills for depression.

Objectives

- A student will become familiar with depression statistics.
- A student will be able to identify several of the leading causes of depression.
- A student will learn at least seven out of ten signs and symptoms of depression.
- A student will be able to identify six activities that can help decrease depression.
- A student will be able to verbalize the seven coping skills for dealing with depressive symptoms.

WHAT IS DEPRESSION?

Depression is an illness, in the same way that diabetes and heart disease are illnesses. It affects the entire body, not just the mind. Everyone experiences it from time to time—it is only when symptoms are severe and lasting that people need professional help. Here are some facts on depression:

- Depression is the most common mental health disorder in the United States.

- As many as one in every 33 children may have depression. The rate of depression among adolescents is closer to that of depression in adults, and may be as high as one in eight. This means that in a classroom of 30 students, 4 may suffer from depression.

- Depression isn't the same as feeling "sad" or "down." It's not a "mood" someone can "snap out of." It's not a character flaw or a sign of a weak personality. It's also nothing to be ashamed of, and it's never anyone's fault.

- Depression affects males and females of all ages, all races, all economic groups. Women, however, suffer from depression twice as much as men do.

- The risk of depression among teenage girls is particularly high. A recent study of young women found that 47 percent had at least one episode of major depression within five years after high school.

- Once a young person has experienced a major depression, he or she is at risk of developing another depression within the next five years.

- Depression can occur following a life-changing experience, such as a divorce, the death of a loved one or friend, a move, or problems within a family.

- Depression is a treatable medical illness, with definite symptoms and effective treatments, and it is successfully treated in more than 80 percent of cases. Unfortunately, two-thirds of children and adolescents with mental health problems don't get the help they need.

- Untreated depression is the No. 1 cause of suicide.

Depression is a treatable medical illness, with definite symptoms and effective treatments.

There is a link between depression and getting into trouble: trouble with drinking, drugs, and/or sex; trouble with social situations at school and/or bad grades; and trouble with family or friends. Depression is the leading cause of alcoholism, drug abuse, and other addictions.

Stress is a common cause of depression, especially during the teen years, which are a time of emotional and social turmoil. Events that would be difficult for anyone can be devastating for adolescents. Such events include:

Events that would be difficult for anyone can be devastating for adolescents.

- Loss of a parent, other family member, or close friend

- Parents' divorce or separation

- A move to a new area

- Family problems: being or feeling neglected, constant conflict with parents and/or siblings, the ongoing feeling that "nobody understands," not measuring up to your parents' expectations

- A breakup with a boyfriend or girlfriend

- Social and/or academic problems at school

- Having an attention, learning, or conduct disorder

- Having a chronic disease or disability that makes you different from everyone else

- Feeling disappointed in yourself and worrying about your future

- Ongoing rejection by other students

- Continued substance abuse

Many people who have depression have an imbalance of the biochemicals in the brain that affect behavior and mood. This imbalance can cause depression even when there are no stressful situations. Because a person's biochemistry is partially determined by genetics, people who have a close relative with depression are more likely to have depression themselves.

In addition, depression may result from the side effects of certain medications, illnesses, or infections. Chronic illness can also lead to depression.

THE SIGNS AND SYMPTOMS OF DEPRESSION

It's important to recognize the signs and symptoms of depression. Often, a person suffering from depression may not know that she has it. Thinking clearly and rationally becomes difficult, and it may be hard for her to believe that she can be helped. Here are the major signs and symptoms of depression:

- You have no interest in things that used to make you happy or that you thought were fun.

- You think no one cares about you, that you're a burden to others, and that you don't deserve to be happy.

- You avoid spending time with your friends and family, and prefer to be left alone.

- You cry a lot, for no particular reason, and are unable to relax.

- Your grades drop drastically, and you have no qualms about challenging teachers and other authority figures.

- You sleep a lot, or have trouble sleeping.

- You gain or lose a significant amount of weight.

- You feel incredibly tired and fatigued.

- Your head and/or stomach hurt much of the time.

- You stop caring about personal hygiene—how your hair looks, which clothes you wear, and so on.

- You begin to act out—you skip school, run away, drive too fast, and/or engage in unsafe sexual behaviors.

- You abuse alcohol and/or drugs.

- You have thoughts about harming your body, death, and suicide.*

You think no one cares about you, that you're a burden to others, and that you don't deserve to be happy.

* If you recognize these symptoms in yourself or a friend, you should confide in an adult you trust or call a crisis hotline listed in your Blue Pages immediately.

HOW DOES DEPRESSION FEEL?

You get angry and irritated a lot. Everything and everyone annoys you. You're so touchy that you lose control for no reason, and you overreact.

When you're depressed, you feel sad all the time. At times, you also feel anxious (jittery) and numb (like a zombie). Depressed people have also described depression in these ways:

- **You feel hopeless about everything.** Nothing seems worth the effort. You think that you are "no good," you have no confidence, and your self-esteem is very low.

- **You're not interested in ordinary pleasures.** Your favorite music, sports, friends, or entertainment no longer interest you. You feel as if there is a glass wall between you and the rest of the world. Basically, you just want to be left alone.

- **You feel that your life is empty.** Depressed people have said that it feels like drowning or suffocating. To make things worse, you feel guilty for feeling that way.

- **You alienate your friends.** While you may not realize that this is happening, your friends notice the changes in you. They want to help, but feel helpless.

- **You have a hard time making decisions.** You also find it hard to concentrate, and you forget things.

- **You get angry and irritated a lot.** Everything and everyone annoys you. You're so touchy that you lose control for no reason, and you overreact.

- **You feel extremely tired most of the time.** You feel like you want to sleep forever.

- **You feel restless, edgy, and you can't sit still.**

- **You think about death often.** Thoughts about suicide go through your head.*

- **Your body hurts.** You have headaches, stomachaches, and other pains that won't go away.

- **Your eating patterns change drastically.** You feel hungry, overeat, and gain weight, or you become uninterested in food and you lose too much weight.

* If you recognize these symptoms in yourself or a friend, you should confide in an adult you trust or call a crisis hotline listed in your Blue Pages immediately.

TALKING ABOUT DEPRESSION

Depression is paralyzing. It makes any action or effort difficult. Nothing seems worth it; the thought of doing anything seems overwhelming.

It may be hard to take the first step out of depression, but you must remember that there are people who care about you, who want to help. Here are a few suggestions on how to begin your journey back:

- **Give yourself permission to feel bad.** Tell yourself that it's okay to cry. Emotions need to be felt, even if they don't feel good. If you can feel your feelings, you can heal them.

- **Face your feelings.** Try to talk about them with a close friend, family member, teacher, or other person whom you trust and with whom you feel comfortable.

- **Try to verbalize your frustration, helplessness, anger, worthlessness, etc.** Remember that you can talk about anything, no matter how unpleasant and embarrassing, with anyone who cares about you.

- **Admitting that you feel bad is the first step toward recovery.** You can say things like:
    - "I'm feeling really bad, and I think I might be depressed."
    - "I'm feeling so down that I don't care about anything any more. I think I need some help."
    - "I know my grades are slipping, but I don't have enough energy to do anything about it. I need to do something to feel better."
    - "I need to tell someone how confused and sad I feel."
    - "Nothing really matters anymore. I wish someone would help me."

- **When you ask for help, it's a sure bet that you'll get it.** Other ways to face your feelings include:
    - When you can't seem to think straight, stop thinking and feel. Becoming aware of your feelings can help you sort through them.
    - When you're afraid, breathe deeply until you calm down. Then find someone you trust to talk to. Keep a list of people you trust, with their home and work phone numbers.
    - When you're angry, talk or write about it instead of acting out.
    - When you're lonely, call or visit someone.

Keep a list of people you trust, with their home and work phone numbers.

HOW TO HELP YOURSELF FEEL BETTER

If you're not ready to discuss your feelings, writing about them can help a lot.

Besides talking about your feelings, there are many things you can do to help yourself feel better. It may be hard to muster the energy and you may feel that you're not deserving, but you won't begin to heal until you do. Here are some suggestions:

- **Pool your human resources.** Accept the love and attention that family members and friends are trying to give you.

- **If medication is prescribed for you, take it faithfully.** You wouldn't hesitate to take an aspirin for a headache, or insulin for diabetes. If an antidepressant could help you feel better, go for it. Once you're on it, try to gauge how much better you feel, and remember how you felt before you began to take it.

- **Make the most of therapy.** You probably don't want to talk to a professional about your depression. You're embarrassed. You can't figure out what's wrong with you. That's the point—the therapist will help you. And in therapy, you can talk about anything at all. It's your time, and you can do what you want with it.

- **Keep a journal.** If you're not ready to discuss your feelings, writing about them can help a lot. They need to be expressed, and many people find it easier to write about how they feel than to talk about it. Writing in a journal takes only a few minutes each day. Or you can use it many times a day if you choose. And you can write about anything you want, because it's your journal.

- **Get your feelings out.** If you're angry, punch a pillow, bounce a ball really hard (outside), or throw a Nerf ball at the wall. Getting rid of your angry feelings in a physical but safe way is therapeutic and it feels great too.

- **Eat right.** Maybe you're not interested in eating, or you're eating so much that you're gaining weight like crazy. You already know that healthy foods give you energy. Eating properly will make you feel better physically and improve your mood.

- **Improve your sleeping habits.** If you have problems falling or staying asleep, take a warm bath or shower before bed. Don't eat or drink anything with caffeine in the evening. Relax by visualizing yourself lying on a beach, or by taking slow, deep breaths and flexing your muscles from head to toe, one at a time.

HOW TO HELP A FRIEND WHO'S DEPRESSED

When you know the signs and symptoms of depression, it's not hard to recognize someone who's depressed. The changes in behavior and actions make her seem like a different person! This can be particularly painful and difficult to handle, and you may begin to wonder why you liked her so much in the first place. But you should not take any offensive behavior personally, because she has an illness and cannot help it.

Most importantly, your depressed friend needs to know that you are there for her—wherever you may be, whenever she needs you. Tell her that. She needs to know that you care about her when she's having a hard time caring about herself, even if you are having a hard time liking her. Here are some other suggestions:

• **Listen, listen, listen.** Don't lecture, criticize, or dismiss her comments. Never tell her to "snap out of it," or that "this feeling will pass." It probably will pass, but it will take time and effort.

• **Encourage your friend to talk about her positive traits,** or ask her to make a list of things that people like about her and why she thinks they feel that way. She should also list things that she does well, and people who think she's pretty great. This may be difficult, as her self-esteem is at an all-time low, but reading the list as often as she wants and keeping it with her will give her a boost when she needs one.

• **If your friend is abusing alcohol or drugs, try to get her to see that these substances are only temporary "fixes."** She probably knows this already, but when you are under the influence of an addictive drug it's hard to admit it. Emphasize the importance of getting help, and help her think of an adult (a parent, teacher, counselor, or clergyperson) who can help her begin to take control of her life.

• **Encourage your friend to go places with you**—to the movies, concerts, ball games, parties, and other events. Don't expect her to say yes at first; in fact, you should expect her to say no. Just the fact that you asked, and that you keep asking, will eventually make her realize that you care and that she is worthy of your friendship and attention.

• **Don't let your friend's depression suck you in: It can be contagious.** You may also feel angry and frustrated because your efforts seem futile. At these times you'll need to talk to someone about your own feelings.

Encourage your friend to go places with you.

HOW CAN I TELL MY PARENTS?

The most important thing is getting help — don't let anything stand in your way.

Parents often have a hard time hearing and accepting that their child is depressed. No parent wants to think that something is wrong with a child, especially something that's a mental illness. Even though they usually have your best interests at heart, they may say things like "What do you have to be depressed about?" They may also tell you that these feelings are a normal part of being a teenager and that they will pass.

Parents may feel guilty or deny your depression because they feel helpless. They can't hug or kiss this hurt away, and they can't put a bandage on it to make it feel better. They may also not understand much about depression. In a recent survey, more than 70 percent of adults believed that a depressed person just needed to "pull her/himself together." It may be up to you to educate your parents. Once you give them the basics, they will most likely be eager to get help for you. They have probably already noticed a change in you, and they'll talk to a doctor or therapist who will set you on the road to recovery.

However, some parents may not be much help. Maybe you feel that you can't talk to them at all, especially about a problem you are having. If your parents have their own problems (with each other, or with addiction or abuse), you'll need to get help on your own. Chances are, you're already used to taking care of yourself. If you're depressed, you will find it hard to do anything good for yourself, but you have to find a way. You can't let depression ruin your life.

Is there another adult with whom you can discuss your depression? Perhaps you have a favorite teacher or coach, or you feel comfortable talking with the school counselor. Maybe you have a relationship with your priest, minister, or rabbi. These are people who can get help for you. They can also talk to your parents in a way that may be difficult for you. If you can't think of anyone, you can go to your family doctor's office or a local mental health clinic. You could also call a crisis hotline. The most important thing is getting help—don't let anything stand in your way.

ACTIVITY: ARE YOU DEPRESSED?

This simple self-test can help you determine whether you are depressed or merely "down in the dumps." If you answer yes to four or more of these questions, and you've felt extremely sad or down for two or more weeks, you may be depressed.

	YES	NO
I feel sad and anxious most of the time.	☐	☐
I feel worthless and/or guilty.	☐	☐
I get angry at the drop of a hat.	☐	☐
My appetite has changed drastically.	☐	☐
I don't enjoy the things I used to like to do.	☐	☐
I have little energy or enthusiasm for anything.	☐	☐
I sleep too little or too much.	☐	☐
It's hard to concentrate and make decisions.	☐	☐
I act out a lot and have problems with self-control.	☐	☐
I prefer to be by myself, away from others.	☐	☐
I have problems with my family.	☐	☐
I have persistent headaches and/or other pains.	☐	☐
I cut classes/skip school.	☐	☐
I've dropped my extracurricular activities.	☐	☐
I drink/do drugs much more than I used to.	☐	☐
I feel hopeless about the future.	☐	☐
I think about hurting myself, death, and suicide.*	☐	☐

* If you answered yes to this question, you should confide in an adult you trust or call a crisis hotline listed in your Blue Pages immediately.

ACTIVITY: THIS IS HOW I FEEL TODAY

Fill in every blank on this worksheet as honestly as you can. See if you feel better when you're finished. If you have difficulty filling in the blanks, this may be a sign that you're depressed.

Today I feel _____ .

I feel this way because _____ .

Everyone thinks I'm _____ .

Even my best friend thinks I'm _____

because _____ .

My parents are _____ .

They think I'm _____ .

I felt particularly good today when _____

_____ .

I felt particularly bad today when _____

_____ .

But I was able to feel better because _____

_____ .

The best thing that happened today was _____

_____ .

It was great because _____ .

The worst thing that happened today was _____

_____ .

But it worked out because _____ .

I did _____ really well today.

Here's what happened: _____

_____ .

I felt good when _____ was nice to me today.

Here's what happened: _____

_____ .

Three things that are good about me are:

1. _____

2. _____

3. _____

RESOLVING FAMILY ISSUES

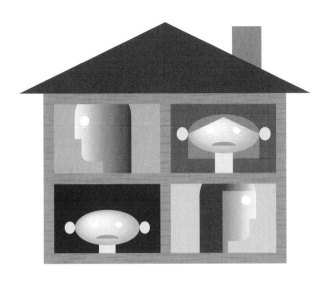

Resolving Family Issues

This chapter offers information about family issues. It discusses the concept of family dynamics and the characteristics of healthy families. It talks about a variety of abuse issues including physical, sexual, and emotional abuse. The chapter offers ways for family members to survive and grow in very difficult situations. There is an activity handout at the conclusion of the chapter to help in recognizing co-dependency issues. A second activity can help raise awareness through art, by drawing the family.

Time Allotment

Two 50-minute sessions integrated into a series of 50-minute class periods.

Goals

To raise awareness of family dynamics that influence how children behave and relate to others. To offer alternative options for family members to utilize when living in difficult family situations.

Objectives

* A student will become familiar with the characteristics of a healthy family.
* A student will be able to list the four major kinds of abuse that can occur in families.
* A student will learn five basic rights that he has as a family member.
* A student will be able to identify six factors that can cause family dysfunction.
* A student will be able to verbalize ways in which he might make changes for himself within his family.

WHAT IS A HEALTHY FAMILY?

When a family functions in a basically healthy way, it is considered to be "functional." Some families, however, function in a disordered or abnormal way, and are sometimes called "dysfunctional." Parents or guardians in functional families strive to provide for their children's emotional and physical needs. In other families, the needs of the children aren't always met. Consequently, these children sometimes have behavioral and psychological problems.

When a family is troubled, tensions are passed along from person to person. Children sometimes begin to feel that they are the reason for the difficulties. This is usually not true, but when children feel this way they learn unhealthy methods to deal with the situation, and thus they begin a destructive cycle that can cause problems throughout their lives.

Here are some destructive patterns that cycle in families:

- **The child is forced to take sides in conflicts.** As a result, he learns quickly that no matter who he sides with, he can't win.

- **The child may be ignored, discounted, or criticized for his thoughts and feelings.** Consequently, he learns to keep them to himself to avoid conflict.

- **The adults may be distant and uninvolved.** Even as a youngster, the child learns to take care of his needs on his own.

- **Too much structure and too many demands are placed on the child's time, choice of friends, or behavior.** Or, they may receive no structure or discipline whatsoever. This child becomes responsible for making his own decisions without support from anyone in the family.

- **The child may experience rejection by one or both parents/ guardians.** Or, he may get preferential treatment over another sibling.

When a family is troubled, tensions are passed along from person to person.

If someone in your family is abusive toward you, keep in mind that you are not alone. Statistics show that:

• Twenty million children grow up in families where alcohol, drugs, or both are abused by at least one parent. In a typical school, at least 20 percent of the students have an alcoholic parent.

• One out of every eight boys and one out of every four girls will be sexually abused before the age of 18. In 90 percent of these cases, sexual abuse will occur in the home. And these are only the reported incidents—many more are unreported and undetected.

There are four major kinds of abuse:

Physical abuse. The following actions are considered physical abuse when they are continuous, pervasive, and extreme, and if a parent or any adult intentionally does them to a child or adolescent and causes injury or pain:

• Hitting
• Throwing
• Kicking
• Choking
• Biting
• Shaking
• Beating with an object
• Burning with a match, cigar, or cigarette
• Scalding with hot water
• Pushing a child underwater
• Tying up a child

Physical neglect. The following actions are considered physical neglect if they interfere with a child's growth and development:

• Not providing adequate housing or warm clothing in cold weather.
• Keeping a child locked in a closet or a room.
• Leaving a child alone for extended periods of time.
• Refusing to provide medical care when a child is sick or injured.
• Placing a child in a physically dangerous situation.

Sexual abuse. The following actions are considered to be sexual abuse if they are done to a child or adolescent by a family member or other adult:

• Fondling, touching, or kissing a child's sex organs.
• Making a child touch someone else's sex organs.
• Having intercourse with a child.
• Showing a child pornographic material.

There are four major kinds of abuse: physical abuse physical neglect sexual abuse emotional abuse.

- Showing a child sex organs.
- Forcing a child to undress.
- Forcing a child to have sex with someone.
- Making a child pose or perform for pornographic pictures or videos.
- Telling a child "dirty" stories.

Emotional abuse. When a parent ignores, terrorizes, blames, belittles, or otherwise makes a child feel that he is worthless and incompetent, that parent is emotionally abusive. Much of the material elsewhere in this module discusses emotional abuse.

Families pass traditions, stories, and memories down through the generations. They can also pass along destructive patterns of functioning that affect all family members. The family members are often unaware of this cycle of destructiveness within their families. The adults in the family are often themselves the victims of such patterns and pass them unconsciously along to their children.

It's important to understand and recognize the factors that can cause a family to function in an unhealthy manner:

• **Children may be pulled into marital conflict.** Whether this is intentional or unintentional, it diverts attention from the real problems and places it onto the children. The children often become scapegoats, and are viewed as the cause of or reason for the problems.

Children are sometimes seen as "possessions" whose primary purpose is to respond to the physical and/or emotional needs of adults.

• **Children can be affected by addictions or compulsions that are out of control.** These negative behavior patterns include drug and/or alcohol abuse, promiscuity, gambling, overworking, and overeating. All have strong and destructive influences on all family members.

• **Physical violence or force is sometimes used as the primary means of controlling the family.** Children may have to witness or be victims of violence, may be forced to participate in punishing siblings, or may live in fear of explosive outbursts.

• **Children are sometimes seen as "possessions" whose primary purpose is to respond to the physical and/or emotional needs of adults.** For example, a child may be expected to protect one parent from the other, or to be a constant source of cheer for a parent who is depressed.

• **Parents and/or caregivers may be unable to provide, or threaten to withdraw, financial or basic physical care for their children.** Similarly, one or both parents may fail to provide their children with adequate emotional support.

• **Authoritarian methods of discipline are used in the family.** Often, such families are rigid and inflexible in most areas of their daily life. This may encompass religious, political, financial, and moral beliefs. Compliance with expectations and rules is expected without question, and those who rebel must suffer consequences.

EMOTIONAL DYNAMICS

Responsible adults are expected to help children feel good about themselves by supporting them emotionally as well as physically. In some families, however, children are not given such support, so they quickly learn to live without it. The children want their parents and/or caregivers to be happy and satisfied, so they—as a matter of survival—learn to be good and do whatever is expected of them.

Healthy emotional growth is often impossible for these children: They are not allowed to voice their opinions and they are expected to meet the demands put upon them. As they retreat into their own world, they live with fear, anger, and shame, and they expend a lot of time and energy in making their lives look "normal" to outsiders.

Children often feel trapped within the family unit. In an effort to protect themselves and avoid feeling bad, they quickly learn to:

- Repress their own needs.
- Be compliant in an effort to be perfect.
- Do nothing to frustrate or anger the parent or guardian.
- Feel responsible for the negative feelings of the parent or guardian.
- Keep their true feelings to themselves, and agree with whatever their parent or guardian says or does.
- Feel that there is something wrong with them, and that they are therefore unlovable.
- Keep their accomplishments to themselves, when they have parents/guardians who cannot accept that their children may be more adept than them (smarter, better at sports, more attractive, etc.).
- Feel that whatever they do is not good enough.
- Lie or cheat to avoid disapproval.
- Take care of their parent or guardian, with the hope that if they do this, the parent or guardian will be better able to take care of them.
- Do whatever it takes to protect their privacy, and be secretive about anything that might allow their parent or guardian to use information against them.
- Tolerate forced physical closeness instead of being allowed to choose to be affectionate.
- Cope with their pain alone, and hide it.

In an effort to protect themselves, children learn to keep their true feelings to themselves, and agree with whatever their parent or guardian says or does.

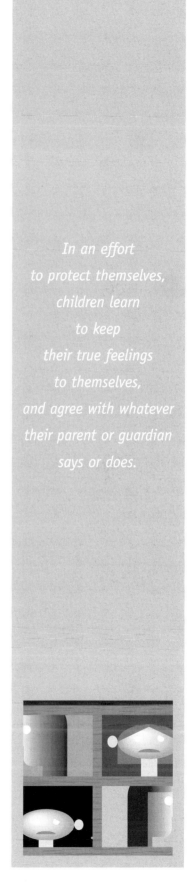

VERBAL ABUSE

"Sticks and stones may break my bones but words will never hurt me" may have been fun to chant during your childhood years, but when you really think about it, the saying is far from true. Words can hurt—a lot.

When children live in families where insults, degrading names, and criticism are common, they absorb extremely negative messages about themselves. Such children grow up expecting to be hurt and humiliated. When they are, somehow it doesn't hurt so much because they have grown used to it.

In other families, members don't listen to each other at all, and this also causes harm. But this section isn't about them—it's about family members who attack each other with words, such as:

Sometimes parents/guardians feel especially threatened when their children begin to look and act like adults (in adolescence).

- **"I'm only saying this for your own good."**
  In order to justify their cruel remarks, the adults try to pass them off as guidance. Even when the child meets expectations, it's never good enough.

- **"You're capable of doing ___, but I doubt you can do it."**
  Some parents/guardians expect the world of their children, but no matter how well the children do, they are constantly put down.

- **"Be your best, but don't be better than me."**
  Sometimes parents/guardians feel especially threatened when their children begin to look and act like adults (in adolescence). No matter how much these adults have, they live in fear of not having enough (perhaps because of the way things were in their childhood), and they constantly compete with their children. When these children do achieve success, they feel guilty instead of feeling proud.

- **"It's your own fault."**
  When statements like this are used within the family context, the members send negative messages to each other. They feel put down and their self-esteem is diminished.

- **"If you do this right, everything will be okay."**
  Parents or guardians who want their children to be perfect are often perfectionists themselves, and they feel that if everything is perfect then everything will be okay. But children in these families are destined to fail, and when they do they become scapegoats for the parents. They think, "If I can't be perfect I might as well give up," and they often do just that—give up.

YOUR RIGHTS AS A FAMILY MEMBER

Parents, guardians, and other caretakers must be role models. They are responsible for instilling a "healthy sense of self" in their children. They do this by fulfilling their children's needs. These include physical needs, such as shelter and food; protection from physical and emotional harm; the need for love, affection, and attention; and ethical and moral guidelines.

In order for children to develop a sense of self-worth, their needs and feelings must be validated. As a child, you have the right to expect certain things of your family. These include:

• **Parental love.** Parental love includes strong affection, tenderness, and devotion to the well-being of one's children. In families where love is scarce and conditional, children do not feel sufficiently cared for, and siblings often compete for attention.

• **Basic trust.** Children should learn in early infancy to trust their caretakers to meet their basic needs with love and consistency. When basic trust isn't established, children become distrustful, and this can lead to feelings of despair and hopelessness.

• **Empathy.** Empathy, the ability to identify with another person's emotional experience, is crucial in a trusting relationship. An empathetic parent or guardian not only listens to what his child has to say, but also tries to understand how he feels. When people feel unaccepted or misunderstood, they do not learn how to be intimate with others. When the other people in their world fail to understand their emotions and needs, they often feel angry and resentful.

• **Parental authenticity.** Parents/guardians should always be honest about who they are. They should admit their mistakes and be quick to repair emotional injuries. They should be able to apologize to their children for overreacting in the heat of the moment, and they should be prepared to let their children see that they are not perfect. In this way, children learn that it's okay to make mistakes. When mistakes are not admitted, children feel confused by the difference between what really happened and what's being said.

• **Social and physical stability.** The emotional development of a family depends on both the quantity and quality of time the family members spend together. When parents are not available, children fail to develop close family relationships. And when children are deprived of the basic necessities of life—adequate housing, health care, and even food—they not only suffer physically; their self-concept is also injured.

The emotional development of a family depends on both the quantity and quality of time the family members spend together.

Change begins with you. You're in control of your life, but you're not in control of other people's lives. You can't make anyone change, but you can make changes in the situations that surround you.

If you're in a family that's set in its ways, it may be very hard to change your behavior. You may feel as if you are completely on your own. And maybe you are. But if you keep the following in mind, you'll be on the road to new relationships:

• **Stop trying to be perfect.** Accept your own faults, and don't try to make others in your family perfect. Remember, you can't change anyone but yourself.

• **Developing awareness.** The first step in creating change is awareness. Think about yourself and how you might react to a situation in your family. Remember, negative emotions are not bad; they're the way you feel, so let them out. Expressing negative feelings may be difficult, especially when family members don't like being confronted and don't want to change. The important thing is not their reaction, but your response. Here are some statements you may encounter, and responses you can offer:

- **Their statement:** "It never happened."
- **Your response:** "Just because you don't remember doesn't mean it never happened."
- **Their statement:** "It was your fault."
- **Your response:** "You can keep trying to make this my fault, but I'm not going to accept responsibility for what you did to me."
- **Their statement:** "I said I was sorry."
- **Your response:** "I appreciate your apology, but that's just a beginning. If you're really sorry, you'll be available to me when I need you."
- **Their statement:** "I'm doing the best I can."
- **Your response:** "I understand that it's hard for you, but you need to know that what you did really hurt me."
- **Their statement:** "Look what I've done for you."
- **Your response:** "I appreciate those things, but they don't make up for the physical/verbal abuse I've had to endure."

• **Identify what you would like to have happen.** Tell the person in clear terms what would make things better/simpler/happier for you.

• **Don't be upset if change doesn't happen immediately.** Lasting change happens gradually. As you continue to practice new and healthier behaviors, they'll begin to feel normal, and they'll result in new and healthier patterns.

IF YOU ARE BEING ABUSED

If you are the victim of abuse, it may be extremely embarrassing to expose this secret, and seemingly impossible to break the cycle.

If you are being physically or sexually abused, you'll need to get help from the outside. It's extremely important to take steps to stop this destructive cycle—now.

Tell a responsible adult to whom you feel close and who can help you. This could be a teacher or counselor; priest, minister or rabbi; a relative; or caring neighbor. If you don't trust any of these people, you should go to or call the local police station or child welfare office, or call a local hot-line listed in the Blue Pages under "Child Abuse."

If one or both of your parents is an alcoholic or a drug abuser, it's important to keep in mind that alcoholism and drug addiction are diseases, and there is nothing you can do to make the person stop. People can change their own lives, but they cannot make other people change.

To make your life more bearable, you may need to get help from people outside your family. The people listed above can be excellent helpers. Consider also calling the local chapter of Alateen, an organization that sponsors meetings for children of alcoholics where they share their feelings and ways of dealing with their problems.

If you are being emotionally abused, it's extremely important to learn how to take care of yourself and build your self-esteem. You can do this by doing things you enjoy away from home, with friends who like you for who you are. Seek people who are willing to listen to you without judging or criticizing, and who can give you advice on how to treat your situation at home.

It's certainly easier said than done, but if you can learn to detach yourself, you can learn to take care of yourself in nurturing ways. Positive experiences and relationships lead to positive feelings about yourself. Eventually, the hurt at home won't seem so devastating.

To make your life more bearable, you may need to get help from people outside your family.

ACTIVITY: BEHAVIOR AWARENESS CHECKLIST

The term "co-dependency" has been used to define relationships in which one person enables the negative behavior of another, or takes responsibility for it. For example, do you find yourself trying to be perfect in order to keep your parent from getting angry with you?

Co-dependency is dangerous because it only perpetuates the bad behavior and feelings—it does nothing to change them. This exercise may prompt you to take a closer look at the dysfunction in the relationship in question.

Check the following behaviors if they describe you:

☐ It's my job to make mom/dad happy.

☐ My good feelings depend on approval from _____.

☐ I protect _____ from the effects of his/her behavior.

☐ I don't pay any attention to how I feel or what I want.

☐ I only care about what _____ feels and what _____ wants.

☐ I will do anything to avoid being rejected by _____.

☐ I will do anything to avoid making _____ angry with me.

☐ I shouldn't do anything that would hurt _____'s feelings.

☐ If _____ would only change, I'd feel better about myself.

☐ There's no point in telling _____ how I feel because it wouldn't do any good.

☐ I would never do anything to show _____ that I'm my own person, with my own voice.

☐ If I confront _____, he/she will cut me out of his/her life.

☐ I feel scared when I'm angry with _____.

☐ I feel angry because I'm afraid of _____'s reactions.

☐ I blame myself for everything that goes wrong.

☐ I feel unappreciated, angry, and used a lot of the time.

☐ I pretend that everything is fine when it isn't.

☐ I feel that I can't do anything exactly right.

ACTIVITY: A PICTURE OF MY FAMILY

On this page, draw a picture of your family. Label each family member. Under each, list the traits and characteristics that make them the unique people they are. Be sure to list negative and positive aspects of their personalities (e.g., funny, angry, loving, depressed, caring, preoccupied). Be as specific as possible, and list as many as you can think of.

When you're finished, think about the negative traits you've listed and how these affect you. Then think about how you can learn to deal with them. Remember, you can't change people, so don't waste time on the "if onlys."

THE EFFECTS OF DIVORCE

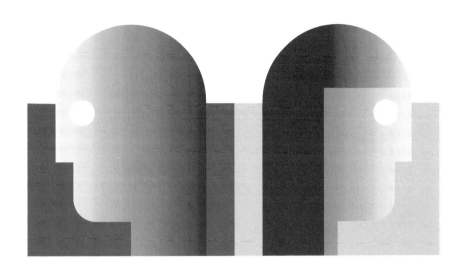

The Effects of Divorce

Divorce is the most common trauma experienced by children and teenagers today. This chapter provides basic but important information about divorce and its effects. It describes the various feelings children may experience when parents divorce and offers coping skills to deal with this loss. It talks about custody and stepfamily issues as well. The activity pages are directed toward helping children of divorce become aware of their feelings.

Time Allotment

Two 50-minute sessions integrated into a series of 50-minute class periods.

Goal

To provide basic but important information about the issue of divorce.

Objectives

- A student will be able to identify at least three effects that divorce has on children.
- A student will be able to talk about the nine most common feelings that occur when parents divorce.
- A student will be able to list two to three coping skills for dealing with divorce in the family.

FACTS ABOUT DIVORCE

Divorce is the most common trauma experienced by American children and teenagers. It is an experience of loss, and its effects are often felt for many years.

For kids, it means dealing with confusion, conflict, change, anger, and sadness, along with the normal challenges of growing up. It often means losing a parent, changing schools or neighborhoods, sharing parents, dealing with parents' dating, adding new family members, and coping with living in two places.

Most children can handle a divorce if both parents continue to be loving and supportive toward them and if both parents do not involve the children in their conflict. It's important for parents to be fair and kind to each other, as hard as that may be for them.

If your parents are divorcing, or if they are already divorced, the following facts can help you understand that you are not alone:

* Every year, there are 1.1 million divorces in the United States. This means that one-third of children today will experience a parental divorce.

* Forty percent of all children in the United States live in a home without a father.

* A recent study determined that 75 percent of children are against their parents' divorce.

* About 10 percent of children report feeling relieved when their parents divorce.

* In nine out of ten divorce cases, mothers are given primary custody of their children. Even when fathers are given weekend visitation, they sometimes do not see their children. A national survey found that 49 percent of children had not seen their fathers once in 12 months, and fewer than one child in six saw their fathers once a week.

* One-third of children have substantial problems in the years following divorce, another third have some moderate adjustment problems, and the final third adjust very well.

* More than 60 percent of "troubled" youth have parents who are divorced or separated.

A national survey found that 49 percent of children had not seen their fathers once in 12 months.

(continued)

(continued)

• It's not the divorce that causes problems for children, but the amount of parental conflict to which children are exposed, the way parents respond to their children during the divorce, and the way they parent their children afterward.

• It's a myth that parents should stay married for the sake of their children. A recent study found that children who live with a divorced parent have fewer problems than those who live with parents who always fight.

• There is an apparent link between divorce and psychiatric problems. Even 10 years after a divorce, 41 percent of children in a recent study were still doing poorly—underachieving, tense, insecure, self-critical, and/or angry.

• Boys seem to have the hardest time dealing with divorce. Many become aggressive, defiant, hard to discipline, and socially insecure. They frequently get into trouble with the police and school authorities.

• Boys aged 12 and older from divorced single-parent families have more conflicts with the law than any other group of the same age.

• Some adolescent girls without a father in the home feel negative toward male adults and peers. When they are with men, they behave in a more sexually provocative way than girls with fathers in the home, resulting in more unwanted pregnancies. They tend to become more aggressive toward parents and peers, and their involvement with drugs and alcohol often increases.

• Some girls react by becoming anxious, withdrawn, or overly well-behaved.

A recent study found that children who live with a divorced parent have fewer problems than those who live with parents who always fight.

WHAT YOU MAY FEEL AND WHAT TO DO ABOUT IT

There are many emotions you may experience before and after your parents get divorced. It's important to remember that all feelings are okay—it's what you do with them that counts.

Shock. When your parents tell you that they are planning to get a divorce, your initial reaction may be one of shock, unless they have been fighting for a while and you suspected that this would happen.
What to do: Even though it will be very hard, you must accept the reality of the situation and move on.

Depression. You may begin to feel frightened, alone, helpless, and hopeless, because you have no control over the events in your life.
What to do: Talk to anyone to whom you feel close and get your feelings out. You'll feel better if you do.

Loneliness. If none or few of your friends have divorced parents, you may feel that nobody understands what you are going through and that you are a burden to your friends. This may lead you to spend more time alone.
What to do: Seek out other kids whose parents are divorced and try to talk with them. You'll find that they are feeling, or have felt, the same way you do.

Denial. In order to cope with the many negative feelings that you may be experiencing, you may develop the defense mechanism of "denial" to protect yourself from such feelings.
What to do: Denying reality is unhealthy. It just postpones the inevitable—feeling the pain. You must get past the denial and accept that your parents are indeed getting divorced.

Anger. In your desire to take control of the situation, you may place blame on an event, yourself, or one of your parents. You may become very angry with your parents because they are no longer there for you.
What to do: Don't try to pin the blame on anyone or anything. Recognize that the divorce is the result of many things combined, and that no one can truly say exactly what caused it. Remember that you are not to blame. You did nothing to cause this situation.

Abandonment. You may feel that your parents have "abandoned" you because they are so involved in the details of the divorce. You may resent the fact that they no longer seem to care about anything else, including you.
What to do: Recognize that this is a very hard time for your parents, just as it is for you. Let them know how you feel. They may be so wrapped up in the divorce that they may not realize that they have distanced themselves from you.

(continued)

Denying reality is unhealthy. It just postpones the inevitable — feeling the pain.

(continued)

Fear. The anger and fighting that your parents are experiencing may be very frightening. You may not have seen your parents like this before. You may feel uncertain and fearful of the future—where you will live, whether you will be forced to take sides, and so on.

What to do: Tell your parents that you need to know the answers to questions such as these, and make sure they provide them.

Low self-esteem. Many kids whose parents are divorced think something is wrong with them, and if they could just "fix" themselves, everything would be all right. Your self-esteem, or the way you perceive yourself, can be drastically reduced by such feelings.

What to do: Keep telling yourself that there is nothing wrong with you just because your parents are divorced, and that fixing things is not an option.

Guilt. Your parents may not adequately explain why they are getting a divorce. As a result, you may begin to think that it's because of you.

What to do: Do not get into the pattern of thinking "If only I had done something differently, or behaved in a different way, this wouldn't have happened." It simply isn't true.

Keep telling yourself that there is nothing wrong with you just because your parents are divorced.

STAND UP FOR YOUR RIGHTS

As your parents go through this difficult time, they may pay less attention to you and they may be less helpful. But even though they are experiencing problems, they are still responsible for your welfare. You need your parents to be there for you just as much as you did before—maybe more—and they need to know this. You also shouldn't feel responsible for trying to make your parents feel better—that's what they should do for you. Keep these ideas from *Good Answers to Tough Questions About Divorce* in mind:

• You have the right to know why your parents are getting a divorce, and to have any questions that you may have answered directly and honestly.

• You have the right to know what your future holds. Ask questions and get answers so that you will feel more secure about what's ahead. If your parents don't know the answers yet, at least they will know that you're concerned.

• You have the right to continue your own life and to attend to your own hopes and needs during this period.

• You have the right not to become caught between your parents as they struggle with each other.

• You have the right to your feelings, whether they feel good or not, and you have the right to express them—and you should!

• You have the right to work through your feelings, whatever it takes, and to receive cooperation from other family members in dealing with any problems you are experiencing.

• You have the right to expect both of your parents to spend time with you. Even if your parents are sad or angry, communicate your need to be with them. If one parent is living in a distant place, you have the right to expect him/her to keep in contact with you.

• You have the right to demand that your parents refrain from bad-mouthing each other to you or using you as an informant. You need to feel that it is okay to love both parents without making anyone unhappy.

• You have the right to be a kid, with your own thoughts, feelings, and worries. You should not internalize the worries and problems of your parents, even if they share them with you. That's for them to work out, not you.

You have the right to a satisfying relationship with each of your parents.

You have the right to expect the same support and resources that have always been provided by your family — at school, in social situations, and help with other decisions.

You have the right to expect your parents to celebrate your birthday, holidays, and other important events with you.

If your parents divorce, the whole family will be in turmoil for a while. Everything will feel "odd" and unfamiliar until a new routine is set. Until things begin to run smoothly, you'll need to take charge of your own life as best you can.

Follow these guidelines for surviving this difficult time:

• **Face the divorce head-on.** Don't try to ignore or deny what is happening. Accept and admit that your parents are getting divorced and that they will probably not get back together again.

• **Get the information you need to feel secure.** You may not be told everything you need to know. Find out the answers to these questions:

- Why did the divorce happen?
- When will the divorce be final?
- What's going to happen to you after the divorce?
- Who will have custody of you?
- Where will you live?
- Who will be living with you?
- When will you see your non-custodial parent?

You may want to explore these questions with each parent separately. If their answers are different, you'll need to talk to an adult outside your family. Talking to a family or school guidance counselor is a good idea.

• **Learn to understand your emotions.** Acknowledge your feelings about the divorce. Keep a journal and write your thoughts and feelings in it. Talk to people who have gone through divorce themselves. It may take a long time, even years, to adjust to your new situation, so keep acknowledging your feelings.

• **Do your best to adjust to your new situation.** It's easy to glorify your old life; to think that things were so much better then. Make a list of the things you didn't like when your parents were living together. Remember the fighting and the tension between them? Anytime you begin to miss the old days, look at the list and be grateful that you don't have to deal with the those problems anymore. Now make a list of the things you like about your new situation. Add to the list every time you discover something you like. Look at this list whenever you need a lift.

Keep a journal and write your thoughts and feelings in it. Talk to people who have gone through divorce themselves.

Make a list of the things you didn't like when your parents were living together.

THE INS AND OUTS OF JOINT CUSTODY

It's likely that your parents will have "joint custody" of you and your siblings. This means that you will be living with both parents for equal amounts of time, or you will be living with one parent most of the time and spending some or all weekends with the other parent. There are other arrangements in joint custody; these are the most common.

Living in two places can be very difficult. Your new home may be very strange and hard to get used to. It may also be hard to live in a new place with just one of your parents. You may feel guilty about feeling more comfortable in your old home than in the new one. You may miss your old neighborhood, and you may not be able to be with your friends as often if the new home is far away. The logistics of having your belongings in both places may be very difficult to work out. And these are just a few of the considerations of joint custody!

Your "other" parent may not want to any spend time at all with you. As sad as this will make you feel, you need to remember that it isn't normal for parents not to stay in touch with their children. Also remember that there is nothing wrong with you; it's your parent who has the problem. Even though parents love their children, they sometimes become so involved with their own problems that they cast the children aside. Parents who don't make an effort to stay in touch usually need professional help. If they get help, there's always the chance that they will realize how hurtful their acts have been.

If you are living in two places, try your best to make your new home as comfortable as possible. Bring some of your favorite stuff over and leave it there. If you can, buy two of certain things so you don't have to keep carrying them back and forth. Keep a list of school and social events and homework due dates at both homes, and make sure your parent knows when and where you need to go, with enough advance planning time. Talk to your friends on the phone as much as you want (within reason!), and invite your friends over. Spend some time alone with your parent; you may enjoy it!

Remember, the ultimate goal is to feel at home in your new home, and not like a guest. After all, your parent isn't new to you, and you're not new to him/her—it's just the surroundings and situation that are temporarily unfamiliar.

If you are living in two places, try your best to make your new home as comfortable as possible.

Keep a list of school and social events and homework due dates at both homes.

LIVING IN A STEPFAMILY

Stepfamilies are the fastest-growing type of family in the United States. Approximately one-half of all divorced adults remarry within one year, and 75 percent of women and 80 percent of men remarry within three years. As a result, about one out of every four children will spend some time living with a stepparent.

There is usually a high level of conflict during the first two years of a remarriage. Tension and resentment are rampant, and it may be hard to get used to new family relationships. Here are some things to remember if you are in—or soon to be part of—a stepfamily:

• **Acknowledge that it is hard to accept that your parent is going to have a new spouse.** It may have been hard for you when your parent dated other people, and this may be much worse. It's okay to be angry about it. Talk to your parent about how you feel.

• **Your parent's new spouse will never replace your biological parent, and he or she shouldn't try to do so.** In the most successful remarriages, the parenting roles remain with the biological parents.

• **Living with stepsisters and stepbrothers may be very difficult.** After all, these are kids you don't know very well and may not like very much. You may be jealous of them, and they may be jealous of you. It's important to acknowledge this and try to work it out. Eventually, you may become friends, or at least begin to like each other.

• **You may resent the time your parent spends with the new spouse or new stepchildren.** It takes time away from you, but remember that your parent has the right to be happy. He or she deserves to have another adult to feel close to.

• **Your relationship with each of your parents should not change just because one of them remarries.** Just because you have a stepmother or stepfather, this doesn't mean that you shouldn't spend as much time with your biological parent as before.

• **You may feel guilty about liking your stepparent.** It may feel as if you are betraying your biological parent if you become close with your stepparent. Think of it this way: You like a lot of people, so isn't it great that one of those people is your stepparent?

• **You may experience difficulty accepting your new stepparent as a disciplinarian.** Complying with an authority figure other than a biological parent can be very difficult. Stepfamilies often leave disciplinary actions to the biological parents. If this is not the case with your family, try talking with your biological parent you live with—to work out a plan that best suits everyone involved.

In the most successful remarriages, the parenting roles remain with the biological parents.

TEN IMPORTANT THINGS TO REMEMBER

1. Divorce is never, ever the child's fault, and it is hardly ever one parent's fault.

2. Your mother will always be your mother, and your father will always be your father, no matter where each one lives, whether they live with you or not.

3. Nothing is wrong with you just because your parents are divorced. You should not feel embarrassed about it, because it has nothing to do with you as a person.

4. Your parents will not get back together if you are on your best behavior. One thing has nothing to do with the other. Thinking up ways to get them back together won't make them do it either.

5. It's always okay to cry, or to get angry. You'll feel better if you do, especially if you express your anger in a positive way, like talking it out. If you have questions, don't be afraid to ask them. You'll find that many people want to help you feel better.

6. Never let your parents put you in the middle of their problems or use you as a messenger.

7. Don't feel guilty if you are feeling happy or having a good time when your parents are feeling bad. It's okay to feel good when others aren't.

8. Wishing you had your old life back is a waste of time. Find ways to feel better about moving on with your life.

9. Just because your parents think it was a mistake for them to marry each other doesn't mean that you can't have a happy marriage of your own some day.

10. In time, your new life will feel as familiar as your old life did. Your feelings of anger and sadness will bother you less and less as time passes.

Just because your parents think it was a mistake for them to marry each other doesn't mean that you can't have a happy marriage of your own some day.

This may seem a strange question, but divorce affects everyone in a family, not just the parents. This questionnaire will help you to determine whether you need some help with the challenges of living through a divorce. If you answer yes to four or more questions, you may want to talk to someone who can help you feel better.

	YES	NO
I feel guilty and/or responsible for the divorce.	☐	☐
I feel guilty because I couldn't stop the divorce.	☐	☐
I keep wishing my parents would get back together.	☐	☐
I've lost part of my childhood because of the divorce.	☐	☐
My parent(s) depend(s) on me for emotional support.	☐	☐
I often have to be a peacemaker when my parents fight.	☐	☐
My parents make me take sides when they fight.	☐	☐
My parents are overly involved with their problems.	☐	☐
My feelings are often overlooked and rarely discussed.	☐	☐
I find it hard to concentrate in school and at home.	☐	☐
My grades have been affected by the divorce.	☐	☐
I have a hard time having fun with my friends.	☐	☐
My friends think I'm weird because my parents are divorced.	☐	☐
I feel angry and/or sad most of the time.	☐	☐
I feel guilty when I feel happy because my parents are sad.	☐	☐
I worry about what will happen to me in the future.	☐	☐
I worry about my mom/dad because she's/he's so sad.	☐	☐
I'm mad because my mom/dad isn't sad about the divorce.	☐	☐
I worry about financial problems caused by the divorce.	☐	☐
I still feel angry even though my parents divorced years ago.	☐	☐
I wonder if my mom/dad still loves me.	☐	☐
I wish my life were the same as it was before the divorce.	☐	☐

ACTIVITY: WHAT WOULD YOU SAY?

Divorce can lead to other problems for everyone involved, especially if it involves a lot of conflict and bitterness. Things may feel really bad for a while. Eventually, however, families are able to rebuild and function again, even though their new life may be very different. Based on what you've learned, what would you say in the following situations?

• Allison's parents have been divorced for a few months, but her mom is still very sad and depressed. Allison wants to help her mom feel better, but doesn't know how. She decides that it's better not to talk about it at all.

Do you agree with Allison? _____ Why or why not? _____

What do you think Allison should do? _____

Why? _____

• Brandon thinks that if he's really good his parents might not get divorced. He keeps his room really neat, does his chores and homework without being reminded, and does anything he's asked to do without complaining. When his parents decide to go through with the divorce, he's furious.

Do you think Brandon was right to think that he could prevent the divorce? _____ Why or why not? _____

Why do you think he felt so angry when his parents told him the news?

_____

• Blair's mom has asked her to find out everything she can about her dad's new girlfriend, and then report back to her with the details.

Do you think Blair should do this? _____ Why or why not? _____

Is it fair for Blair's mother to ask this of her? _____
Why or why not? _____

ARE YOU ASSERTIVE?

Are You Assertive?

This chapter focuses on helping children to be assertive in their interactions with others. The chapter begins with explaining the three different personality types—passive, assertive, and aggressive. The remainder of the chapter provides skills to increase assertive behavior through easy-to-read formulas, role-plays, and strategies. Teaching children to make "I" statements rather than placing blame on the other person emphasizes clear communication. The activities at the end of the chapter offer continued practice in clear communication and distinguish between what is assertive and what is not.

Time Allotment

Two 50-minute sessions integrated into a series of 50-minute class periods.

Goals

To learn to differentiate between passive, aggressive, and assertive methods of communicating. To learn and develop basic assertive principles to enhance interactions with others and increase self-esteem.

Objectives

- A student will be able to identify whether he is passive, aggressive, or assertive.
- A student will be able to list the six components of the A.S.S.E.R.T. formula.
- A student will be able to verbalize five out of ten strategies for learning to express feelings.
- A student will learn how to use "I" messages when communicating.

ARE YOU PASSIVE, AGGRESSIVE, OR ASSERTIVE?

You have many needs—for love, friendship, respect, understanding, and the freedom to make decisions that will affect the way you live. How will you make sure your needs are met? Sticking up for yourself is important, because most of the time no one else will do it for you. Which of these three common personality types is yours?

Passive. When you're passive, you fail to openly and honestly express your thoughts, and feelings. You allow your rights to be violated by others, and people tend to ignore you. People don't take you seriously, and it's obvious to others that you have little respect for yourself. Passive behavior says "You count, and I don't." When you're passive, you:
- Don't speak up for yourself.
- Don't say what you really mean.
- Speak softly, in a timid voice.
- Don't make eye contact with others.
- Apologize for bothering the person you're talking to.

Aggressive. When you're aggressive, you express your thoughts, feelings, and beliefs in a way that violates the rights of others. Your goal is to dominate and win regardless of what others think of you. Your actions are often inappropriate and show a clear lack of respect for others. What's more, you don't care how others see you. Aggressive behavior says "I count, and you don't." When you're aggressive, you:
- Try to intimidate others with your actions and words.
- Stand with your hands on your hips in an intimidating manner.
- Speak in a loud voice, making demands and accusations.
- Glare at and bully the other person.
- Never back down.

Assertive. When you're assertive, you express your thoughts, feelings, and beliefs in direct, honest, and appropriate ways that do not violate the rights of others. Your messages do not humiliate, degrade, or dominate others. You share your feelings without being embarrassed or ashamed, and you can negotiate with others to get your needs met. You are confident enough to say no, and to refuse to do things you don't want to do. People respect your needs, and you respect theirs. Assertive behavior says "We both count." When you're assertive, you:
- Stand or sit comfortably.
- Make eye contact, and state your needs clearly.
- Use "I" messages and active listening.
- Say what you mean and mean what you say.
- Show by your body language, facial expressions, and tone of voice that you're confident and self-assured.

THE A.S.S.E.R.T. FORMULA

Assertiveness is a skill that can be learned. When you've mastered it, you'll be able to get your needs met, express your feelings, and respond appropriately whenever you feel your rights are violated. Psychologist Earl Hipp's **A.S.S.E.R.T. formula** is designed to help you keep the components of assertiveness in mind:

ATTENTION. You have to get the person's attention before you can work on a problem you're having with him. You have to get him to listen to you, and be sure he is willing to really hear what you have to say.

SOON, SIMPLE, SHORT. As soon as you feel that your rights have been violated, you should respond in a simple manner, keeping it short and to the point.

SPECIFIC BEHAVIOR. Focus on the other person's behavior, not how you feel about him.

EFFECT ON ME. As soon as you've determined how the person's behavior has affected you, communicate this to him. Remember to use "I" statements.

RESPONSE. Determine what you need for the relationship to work (the changed behavior that would help you get along better), and then ask the person for feedback on your request.

TERMS. If all goes well, you should be able to work out an agreement concerning how to handle similar situations in the future.

Here's an example of the **A.S.S.E.R.T. formula** in action:

The problem: *Your best friend Pam is always making decisions for the two of you. She never asks what you want to do.*

A: Pam, can we talk about something that's been bothering me?
S: I'm having a problem with you making all of the decisions about where we go and what we do.
S: It seems like you think I don't have an opinion and that I'm happy to just go along with you. But I would like to have a say in what we do.
E: It feels like my opinion doesn't count for much, and that feels bad.
R: How about if you call me first next time, or if I come up with an idea and ask you about it?
T: This is great. From now on, the best thing would be to take turns deciding what we'll do.

STAND UP FOR YOURSELF

Do you have trouble saying no? Do your friends pressure you to do things you don't want to do, like smoke and drink? Do they expect you to go along with them, even though their plans don't feel right to you?

You don't have to be a passive follower, and you don't have to be an obnoxious aggressor either. If you know what to say and how to say it, you'll find that people will not only listen to you, they'll also respect what you say. Standing up for yourself will get you what you want without hurting others.

Here are examples of passive, aggressive, and assertive responses to several situations:

Situation: You're at a party with friends. A joint is being passed around. You don't want to smoke, so when it comes to you, you pass it to the next person. Your friend says, "Hey, don't you want to get high?"
Passive response: "Oh, well, I guess. Pass it back."
Aggressive response: "If I wanted to, I would, wouldn't I?"
Assertive response: "I don't want to because I don't get high. Thanks anyway."

Situation: You're with your best friend and her boyfriend on the way home from a movie. They decide to park and make out. You're stuck in the back seat.
Passive response: Say nothing at all and wait until they're finished and decide to take you home.
Aggressive response: "You two are so selfish. You never think of anyone but yourselves. Do you think I want to sit here and watch you make out?"
Assertive response: "Can you guys take me home first? Thanks."

Situation: Your friend asks you to let her see your paper during a math test.
Passive response: "We might get caught, but okay."
Aggressive response: "Are you crazy? We could get 'Fs' for that. What a stupid idea!"
Assertive response: "I'd like to help you, but we might get caught. Let's study together and hopefully we'll both do well."

You may have a parent or other role model who is content to sit back and let others take charge. Some people are so used to being in the background that they never question whether life would be better in the foreground. This can be dangerous—these people may be giving up a basic human right: the right to be heard and respected.

Pay attention to the communication patterns in your household, and decide whether they are healthy or dysfunctional.

As a person, you have many basic rights. If you act on these rights, you'll be able to handle conflict in a positive manner, and learning to be assertive will be much easier. These rights include:

- The right to say what you want to say and be heard.

- The right to ask for what you need.

- The right to attempt to influence others.

- The right to disagree and to try to reach a compromise.

- The right to have your own point of view.

- The right to make mistakes, and the right to admit your mistakes.

- The right to bring attention to yourself when you want and need something.

- The right to make a decision and then change your mind.

- The right to judge your own thoughts and feelings, and the right to judge those of others.

- The right to resist other people's judgments.

- The right to stand up for yourself.

- The right to say no.

- The right not to have to justify your opinions, thoughts, and feelings.

- The right to have your limits respected.

While your rights are important, so are those of others. If expressing your rights truly hurts someone else, or if doing so breaks one or more rules, you may have to pull back a bit. But never forget that you deserve to say what you feel, that your ideas and opinions are worthwhile, and that you are strong enough to defend them.

DON'T BLAME, EXPLAIN

A wise observer once summed up the basis of assertiveness: *Don't blame, explain.* If you have trouble expressing your feelings and opinions, you can learn how to stand up for yourself using these basic strategies:

- **Think about what you want and need.** Take some time to sit down and make a list of qualities that you would like to possess. Determine the obstacles that may prevent you from achieving your goals and needs.

- **When you're in a sticky situation, think about how you really feel.** Think to yourself, "This makes me really mad" or "I'm so embarrassed." Then think about what you'd like to have happen: "I want to punch a pillow" or "I want to crawl under a rock." Even though you may not be able to do those things at that moment, it's good to think about what you'd do if you could.

- **Try to determine why you feel that way.** If you're really mad, what can you do about it? If you're really embarrassed, how can you avoid the situation from happening again?

- **Find a good time to describe your feelings.** Use "I" messages instead of blaming others—"I feel angry" rather than "You're so inconsiderate." See page 127 for more information on "I" messages.

- **Connect your feeling with a specific behavior.** For example, say "I was angry because you blabbed my secret," or "I was so embarrassed when you told everyone I'm scared of the dark."

- **Be direct.** Make sure you deliver your message to the person for whom it's intended. Telling everyone else how mad or embarrassed you are won't solve the problem.

- **Don't assume that you know how another person is feeling or thinking.** Maybe he didn't mean to make you angry or embarrass you. Maybe he is truly sorry. Find out why he did it before you decide to stay mad. Chances are that he simply made a mistake.

- **Avoid sarcasm and absolutes.** If someone tries to apologize, accept the apology and don't counter with, "Oh yeah, I'm sure you're sorry. Hah!" You don't want to put the other person on the defensive, because he could turn around and stay mad at *you.*

- **Ask for feedback.** Ask, "Do you know what I mean?" Also ask, "How do you see it?" This will correct any misconceptions you have, and show that you're open to communication.

- **Most importantly, be willing to compromise.** If you don't get all your needs met, meeting halfway isn't half bad.

Although we don't often notice it, the way we communicate is key to how well we get along with others. Clear communication depends on:

• Not putting the other person on the defensive
• Getting your message across
• Really hearing the other person's message

"You" messages accuse the other person: "*You* did this, *you* didn't do that." They also find fault: "It's *your* fault," and they put the other person down: "Why do *you* have to be such a slob?!" Most importantly, they make people feel they're being attacked and they almost always start fights.

Consider this fight between a teen and her mother:

Mother: *"Where have you been young lady? It's almost 1 a.m., and you were supposed to be home at 11! I knew I couldn't trust you. You're so irresponsible!"*
> **Mother attacks with "you" message.**

Daughter: *"You always attack me! I'm late this one time and you make a federal case out of it. You aren't even giving me a chance to explain!"*
> **Daughter counterattacks with "you" message.**

Mother: *"You always have excuses! I can't listen to them anymore. You don't care about anyone but yourself, do you?"*
> **Mother denies daughter's "you" message and counterattacks with another one.**

Daughter: *"You're the one who doesn't care. All you do is yell at me, and you never trust me! You never listen to my side of the story."*
> **Daughter denies mother's "you" message and comes up with another of her own.**

Mother: *"Don't talk to me like that! I've had all I'm going to take from you. That's it—you're grounded!"*
> **Communication breaks down.**

As you can see, "you" messages do not foster communication. Mother and daughter are both on the defensive, angry with each other, and not thinking about how the other is feeling. Most of the time, "you" messages aren't even 100 percent true—they generalize using words like "always" and "never," and they are usually hurtful. With "you" messages, the two parties become so caught up in defending themselves that there's little chance of hearing the other person's side of the story, or learning anything for the future.

"I" MESSAGES

"I" messages are much more effective than "you" messages. They let the other person know how you're feeling, and they are much less likely to make him feel attacked, put down, or angry. They don't talk about what "always" or "never" happens, and they don't make hurtful criticisms. They address the specific situation, and they get your message across, clearly and effectively.

"I" messages usually encompass three steps. They describe (1) the situation without using the word "you," (2) how you felt at that time, and (3) why you felt that way.

Let's look again at the fight the mother and daughter on the previous page were having. Using "I" messages, it isn't a fight at all. Here's how it could have played out using "I" messages:

Mother: *"I've been so worried about you. When it got past 11 and I didn't know where you were, I didn't know what to do."*
> **Mother tells how she felt with an "I" message.**

Daughter: *"I'm really sorry you were so worried. I thought you would be, but I couldn't get to a phone. We were stuck in traffic on the freeway. There was a big accident and the cars were backed up for miles."*
> **Daughter explains with an "I" message.**

Mother: *"Well, the important thing is that you're home safe and sound. I'm so relieved."*
> **Mother communicates that she understands with an "I" message.**

Daughter: *"If anything like this happens again, I promise I'll try harder to call you."*
> **Daughter hears that she has been understood and pledges to be more considerate in the future with an "I" message.**

Mother: *"That would be good. I'm going to think about getting you a cell phone."*
> **Mother comes up with a solution and communicates it with an "I" message.**

You can see how much more calm and satisfying this "I" message conversation is than the "you" message fight on the previous page. Because she didn't feel attacked, the daughter didn't feel the need to counterattack. And because the mother knew the problem was not intentional, she was able to discuss it in a rational manner. The "I" messages helped communication, and a fight was avoided.

EIGHT GREAT WAYS TO SAY NO

Resisting pressure from your friends and other peers can be really hard. You need to be able to say no without backing down or resorting to bullying in return. Even if you're teased or threatened, you have to stand your ground. Here are eight suggestions for saying no to things you don't want to do:

1. Just say no. You can simply say "No, thanks" and walk away.

2. Say no and give a reason. Is the person suggesting something that's dangerous? If it's something that could really get you into trouble, remind the person of the consequences.

3. Say no and change the subject. You could say something like "No, thanks, I'm not interested. Can you believe what Danielle said in class yesterday?"

4. Say no and offer an alternative. Tell the person you can't, and ask him to do something else with you.

5. Say no and ask a question. Say "No thanks. I don't like the way I feel when I smoke. Do you?"

6. Say no and use humor. Try to be funny with a response such as "It would be safer if we played in traffic, don't you think?"

7. Say no and pass a mild judgment. If you say "I thought you were smarter than that," you're not criticizing, you're making the person think about what he's doing, and letting him know that you care.

8. Say no and keep repeating yourself. If someone is putting pressure on you to do something you don't want to do, just say "No, I don't want to" after every argument he uses to convince you. After a while, this will get pretty boring and the pressure will be lifted. But don't give up until you've won the battle.

ACTIVITY: "YOU" vs. "I" MESSAGES

Here's a list of "you" messages parents and kids give each other. Notice how many of them use "always" and "never" generalizations. Notice also how much they put the other person down. Next to each one, write an "I" message. Next time you get into a dispute with your parents, use the appropriate "I" message and see what happens.

"YOU" MESSAGE   **"I" MESSAGE**

Why don't you ever listen to me?   I'd like to talk to you.

What's wrong with you?

When are you going to grow up?

You're so lazy!

You should know better than that.

Why don't you act your age?

You only think of yourself.

You don't care about me at all.

I knew I couldn't trust you.

Can't you do anything constructive?

You never think about what I want.

Everything has to be your way.

Why do you get to make the rules?

You never give me a chance to explain.

You're always on his/her side.

You don't understand me.

Why can't you be more mature?

You never trust me to do anything.

You never listen to me!

You always treat me like a baby.

ACTIVITY: ARE YOU ASSERTIVE?

Assertiveness is a skill that can bring you personal success. If you answer false to more than half of these questions, you may have to go through this chapter again to gain additional perspective on becoming more assertive.

TRUE   FALSE

☐ ☐ It's easy for me to accept a compliment.

☐ ☐ I find it easy to tell someone that I like him/her.

☐ ☐ I don't let people take advantage of me.

☐ ☐ I feel confident when I talk to authority figures.

☐ ☐ I feel secure when I share my feelings.

☐ ☐ It doesn't bother me to express my opinions.

☐ ☐ I can handle aggressive people.

☐ ☐ If I'm not happy with a situation, I take action.

☐ ☐ I have nothing to lose by asking for what I want.

☐ ☐ I feel comfortable saying no.

☐ ☐ If I don't want to do something, I speak up.

☐ ☐ I am able to express my disagreement with a friend.

☐ ☐ I never assume responsibility for others' mistakes.

☐ ☐ If I think someone is wrong, I tell him/her.

☐ ☐ I rarely avoid confrontation.

☐ ☐ I feel and act self-confident.

☐ ☐ I don't feel threatened by assertive people.

☐ ☐ I rarely get caught up with "should haves."

☐ ☐ I do my best to stand up for myself.

UNDERSTANDING EATING DISORDERS

Understanding Eating Disorders

Eating disorders are on the rise in the United States. This chapter provides the alarming statistics on eating disorders for both male and female teens. It provides an overview of both anorexia and bulimia, the two most common eating disorders. Patterns often seen within families are discussed and suggestions for helping someone whom has an eating disorder are offered. There are two handouts at the conclusion of the chapter that can be helpful in evaluating whether someone may have problems with food or body image.

Time Allotment

Two 50-minute sessions integrated into a series of 50-minute class periods.

Goal

To offer information to students on the topic of eating disorders that includes the warning signs of anorexia nervosa and bulimia, the causes of eating disorders, and other issues surrounding these complicated illnesses.

Objectives

- A student will become familiar with the statistics about eating disorders.
- A student will be able to list at least five characteristics of anorexia nervosa and bulimia.
- A student will be able to verbalize four familial patterns associated with children who have an eating disorder.
- A student will identify four to five coping skills to deal with an eating disorder.

STATISTICS AND FACTS ON EATING DISORDERS

Have you heard the saying "You can never be too rich or too thin?" Do you think it's true? Chances are you do, if you're like most young adults. Our society has long promoted slimness as the ideal. It's no wonder the number of anorectic and bulimic teens has skyrocketed.

- It is estimated that 10 percent to 15 percent of American girls aged 14 to 25 suffer from eating disorders.

- One in 200 girls in the United States between the ages of 12 and 18 will develop anorexia.

- More than 70 percent of girls in the United States are dissatisfied with their bodies and want to lose weight.

- In a study of children aged 8 to 10, approximately half the girls and one third of the boys were dissatisfied with their size.

- Anorexia is 10 times more common in girls than in boys. This may be due to the fact that girls are more prone to mood disorders and are more concerned about body shape.

- About 6 percent of anorectics are adolescent boys.

- In a study of girls aged 9 to 15, slightly more than half reported exercising to lose weight, slightly less than half reported eating less to lose weight, and approximately one out of 20 reported using diet pills or laxatives to lose weight.

- Girls who participate in competitive sports where body shape and size are a factor (ice skating, gymnastics, crew, dance, for example) are three times more likely to develop eating disorders. Boys who participate in similar sports, or in wrestling, are also at increased risk.

- In one survey, 29 percent of female eighth-graders said they considered vomiting an acceptable way to lose weight.

- Eighty percent to 90 percent of these patients respond to treatment, but only half of people with serious eating disorders recover completely (coming within 90 percent of normal body weight for age and height).

- Approximately 20 percent to 60 percent of these patients have a chronic eating disorder that redevelops whenever the individual is placed in a stressful situation.

- Approximately 10 percent of anorectics will die of starvation or related problems, including hypothermia, kidney failure, irreversible hypoglycemia, and pulmonary tuberculosis.

Nearly half of all teenagers in the United States know someone with an eating disorder.

Bulimia is thought to be more prevalent than anorexia. Some estimates show that almost 20 percent of girls between the ages of 17 and 25 are bulimic.

A young woman with anorexia is 12 times more likely to die than other girls her age without anorexia.

ANOREXIA NERVOSA: THE "GOOD GIRL" DISORDER

Eating disorders are most common in adolescent girls. They can occur in people who are underweight, normal weight, or overweight. A major factor is the teenage desire to be like teen idols and magazine models. The development of anorexia follows a typical pattern: All of a sudden, a bright, seemingly happy, high-achieving adolescent who is rational in every other way will decide that she's too fat and that 90 pounds is the ideal weight for her 5'4" frame. She begins to skip meals and take diet pills and diuretics, denying her body the nutrients it needs to develop normally. She loses weight quickly but continues to think she's fat. Eventually, she becomes so undernourished that she needs to be admitted to the hospital.

Individuals with anorexia often come from white, middle- to upper-middle-class families that place heavy emphasis on high achievement, perfection, rigid eating patterns, and physical appearance. Many of them feel a need for parental approval as well as a need to achieve some form of independence. These young people often find that controlling their eating patterns is an easy way to assert this independence.

Individuals with anorexia are described by their parents as "model children," because they are obedient, compliant, and good students.

The families of children with anorexia are described as warm and loving on the surface. But members of these families are often excessively involved in each other's lives and overly dependent on one another. They either deny that conflicts exist, or they obsess about petty things so that they are unable to recognize real problems. Children in these families go to great lengths to hide their eating disorders, avoiding wearing shorts, short sleeves, and swimsuits. They wear bulky clothes, and invent excuses to be absent at mealtime.

Anorexia nervosa can lead to life-threatening problems including:

* Low blood pressure, slow pulse, and low body temperature
* Heart rhythm disturbance
* Anemia, menstrual irregularities, and possible infertility
* Failure to menstruate, which can lead to serious thinning of the bones (osteoporosis) that may be permanent
* Failure to grow normally, resulting in shorter stature
* Failure of vital organs, and sometimes, death

About half of the people who suffer from eating disorders will recover, but it's often a long and difficult process. They must re-establish normal eating patterns while they work on psychological problems and family conflicts. Long-term therapy and family therapy may be necessary, and full recovery may take three to four years or even longer.

THE CHARACTERISTICS OF ANOREXIA NERVOSA

Anorexia nervosa is a serious, life-threatening disorder characterized by deliberate self-starvation. The person becomes obsessed with food, weight, counting calories and computing fat content of food, and vigorous exercise.

Physiological characteristics
- Low body weight (loss of at least 25 percent of original weight)
- Slow heart rate
- Low blood pressure
- Reduced body temperature; sensitivity to cold
- Cold hands and feet
- Loss of menstrual period (females); reduced testosterone levels (males)
- Lowered resistance to infection
- Growth of body hair
- Dizziness
- Muscular weakness

Behavioral characteristics
- Excessive dieting, food control, and fasting
- Compulsive exercising
- Insomnia and early morning wakening
- Lack of concentration; confused thinking
- Layering of clothes due to low body temperature and attempt to hide extreme weight loss
- Food rituals: cutting food into tiny pieces, playing with food on plate
- Willingness to cook for family but refusing to eat what is made
- Frequent weighing
- Tension at mealtime, sometimes refusing to eat with family

Emotional/cognitive characteristics
- Dissatisfaction with body in spite of excessive weight loss
- Perfectionism, particularly about physical appearance
- Intense fear of becoming fat
- Depression and irritability
- Tendency to be self-centered and isolated from others
- Distorted body image
- Low sense of self worth
- Denial that anything's wrong

THE CHARACTERISTICS OF BULIMIA

Unlike anorectics, bulimics are usually aware that their eating habits are abnormal, so they hide their behavior.

Bulimia is an eating disorder that is characterized by episodic binge eating followed by purging (vomiting). Binges may be planned or spontaneous, and they typically last from one to two hours, during which as many as 15,000 to 20,000 calories may be consumed. Preferred foods are those that are "forbidden"—cake, pastries, ice cream, and bread.

After the binge period, bulimics are overcome by guilt and shame. Purging rids their bodies of the food and helps minimize the tension that the bingeing generated. But the guilt lingers, and as the process repeats itself, bulimics become victims of their abnormal eating behaviors. They repeatedly try to lose weight by going on severely restrictive diets or using diet pills or diuretics.

The families of bulimics have been characterized as conflicted, chaotic, belittling, and less trusting and nurturing than those of anorectics. They express more anger, and have more addictive behaviors. Mothers of bulimics tend to be depressed and hostile, and fathers tend to be irritable, impulsive and alienated from their bulimic children. Unlike anorectics, bulimics are usually aware that their eating habits are abnormal, so they hide their behavior. Because they are of generally normal weight, their problem can go undetected for years. But their behaviors can lead to a variety of serious health problems:

- Chronic vomiting can lead to bleeding in the throat and can rupture the esophagus.

- Use of syrup of ipecac (to induce vomiting) can cause major damage to the nervous system and the heart.

- Use of laxatives (to purge calories) can lead to bowel problems.

- Vomiting and laxative and diuretic use can result in a serious condition called hypokalemia, in which the body uses too much potassium. This condition can cause the heart to stop.

- Binge eating can lead to obesity, which is associated with high blood pressure, diabetes, high cholesterol, heart disease, arthritis, and some cancers.

FAMILIES AND EATING DISORDERS

Eating disorders are not usually the result of a single factor, but of a combination of social, environmental, and biological factors often including the person's family. While the family can't be blamed for an adolescent's eating disorder, certain patterns of family relations are often associated with these problems.

Enmeshment occurs when family members are so close to each other that they lose their individual boundaries. They may complete each other's sentences, speak for each other, and do things for each other thinking that they are helping each other. For example, a mother will buy her daughter's clothes long past the time when the daughter can make her own decisions about what she wants to buy. Or when the daughter is asked how she is, the mother will answer "Fine," even if the daughter is not fine. Fathers in such families are often emotionally removed from all but one of the members.

Overprotection occurs when a family's natural inclination to protect its members is exaggerated. The family is considered the only safe group, and the world outside is seen as dangerous and untrustworthy. This makes it difficult for children to take risks that will help them gain self-confidence. Children in these families feel they have to protect the family from outsiders and fail to form healthy relationships with others.

Rigidity occurs when a family is resistant to change and will do anything to keep things the way they are. Change is seen as threatening, and being "in control" is valued. There is a fear that sharing of feelings or admission of conflict may lead to upheaval. Even when there is a serious problem such as an eating disorder, there is denial of the need for change.

Reversal of roles can evolve as the affected adolescent often assumes the parents' role of keeping the family together. This often means stepping into the parents' conflicts as a mediator, becoming a confidant for one parent or assuming an adult-like role in the family.

Certain patterns of family relations are often associated with these problems.

JUSTIFYING AN EATING DISORDER

Anorectics and bulimics spend much time trying to justify their behavior. They will use any excuse to convince themselves that what they are doing is right. They tend to think in black and white, and they are very self-centered. Here's what they might say to themselves:

"I'm so gross. I can't even look in the mirror. I'm surprised anyone can look at me."

"Why can't I control myself? I promised myself I wouldn't eat everything, and I did. I'm so weak."

"The only way I can be in control is through eating."

"I'm special/pretty/in control if I'm thin."

"When I used to eat carbohydrates, I was fat. I have to stop eating them now so I won't become obese."

"When my weight was 'normal,' I wasn't happy. So I already know that gaining weight won't make me happier."

"Gaining five pounds would push me over the brink."

"I've gained two pounds. I can't wear shorts anymore. I'm too fat."

"If others comment on my weight, I won't be able to stand it, unless they tell me I look great."

"If I'm not in complete control, I lose all control. I must master this area of my life."

"If I gain one pound, I'll keep going and gain 100 pounds."

"Those people were whispering about me. They probably think I look unattractive. Of course I do—I have gained three pounds."

"I'm embarrassed when other people see me eat."

"Whenever I see a fat person, I worry that I will be like her."

"If I eat something sweet it will immediately be converted into fat."

GETTING HELP FOR AN EATING DISORDER

If you have an eating disorder, the sooner you get help, the sooner you'll begin to feel better about yourself. Here are some important things to keep in mind:

- The most important step in getting help is admitting you have a problem and deciding that you are ready to deal with it.

- Tell yourself that you are good enough, and that you deserve to be happy. Being thin is not a guarantee of happiness or the admiration of others.

- Your happiness does not depend on your weight loss or gain.

- Never be afraid to ask for help.

- Get the people in your family and your close friends to really listen to you. Don't assume that they will somehow know what you want. Try to express your true feelings.

- Seek professional help. Most people are helped with a combination of:
    Medical care and monitoring, which helps to correct and prevent some of the dangerous complications of eating disorders, such as bone density loss and heart problems
    Psychotherapy, which helps to identify the problems that caused the disorder and change the behaviors
    Family counseling, involving your entire family and their unique behavior patterns and dynamics
    Nutritional counseling, which helps you develop a reasonable plan for eating
    Medication, such as antidepressants, which help to readjust the chemistry in your brain that might be partially responsible for the eating disorder

- Self-help groups can offer support from people who are experiencing similar feelings and behaviors, and interaction with people who have successfully overcome eating disorders.

- Places to get help include your family physician, local hospitals, college health services, eating disorder hotlines, and counseling centers.

- Remember that, with help, your chances of getting better are very good. Eighty percent to 90 percent of patients respond to treatment— if not right away, then by the end of two years.

The most important step in getting help is admitting you have a problem and deciding that you are ready to deal with it.

If a loved one or close friend has an eating disorder, your role is to offer ongoing support. Keep these important things in mind:

- Tell the individual you are concerned. Make it clear that you really care and would like to help.

- If you are a parent, become aware of the strong impact you have on your child as her role model. If you're not confident about your own body image, you may pass your insecurities on to your children.

- Suggest that the individual seek professional help. If she refuses, encourage reaching out to an adult such as a teacher, school nurse, or counselor.

- Do not discuss weight, the number of calories being consumed, or particular eating habits. Try to talk about things other than food, weight, calories, and exercise. Encourage talking about feelings instead.

- Avoid commenting on the person's appearance. Concern about weight loss may be interpreted as a compliment, and comments regarding weight gain may be perceived as criticism.

- Never force an anorectic person to eat or a bulimic to stop purging. Remember that the behaviors of anorectics and bulimics are symptoms of emotional problems. They are not doing anything to specifically hurt you.

- Learn all you can about eating disorders.

- Remember that anorectics and bulimics do not choose to do this to themselves. It is a coping mechanism, a means for dealing with depression, stress, and self-hate that have been building for years.

- Encourage the person to move toward self-love while continuing to provide support and encouragement.

- Remember that, ultimately, the responsibility and decision to accept help and to make changes rest with the individual who has the problem.

Remember that anorectics and bulimics do not choose to do this to themselves.

ACTIVITY: MY POSITIVE BODY TRAITS

No one has a perfect body. Everyone has flaws, and what's pleasing to one person isn't always attractive to another. Everyone likes certain things about their bodies, and dislikes other physical traits.

Fill in the blanks on this page. Be honest, and don't be embarrassed or think you're bragging if you give yourself a compliment. Everyone needs to feel self-confident.

Five things I like about my body:

Example: I like being tall because it helps me stand out in a crowd.

1. _____

2. _____

3. _____

4. _____

5. _____

Now fill in these blanks. Think about the reasons why you would like to make the changes, and whether it's realistic to try to change them.

Five things I'd like to change about my body:

1. _____

2. _____

3. _____

4. _____

5. _____

Select the number that best reflects your answer to the following questions and write it in the adjacent box.

4 = *always*
3 = *often*
2 = *sometimes*
1 = *rarely*
0 = *not at all*

Do you think not eating is a healthy method of dieting? ☐

Have you been on several diets during the past year? ☐

Do you eat in secret or hide food? ☐

Does being "fat" frighten you? ☐

Does your self-image depend on what you haven't eaten? ☐

Does eating make you feel ashamed or guilty? ☐

Are you uncomfortable with meals that offer lots of food? ☐

Do you strongly dislike your body? ☐

Do you like to cook for others but not for yourself? ☐

Do you weigh yourself several times a day? ☐

Does your daily exercise regimen take more than two hours? ☐

Do you exercise even when your body is exhausted? ☐

Do you feel better about yourself when you're starving? ☐

Is food your "friend?" Do you eat to feel better? ☐

Do you think you're too fat to be seen in public? ☐

Do you think using laxatives or vomiting are
acceptable methods of weight control? ☐

Do you often gorge yourself with food? ☐

Have you used laxatives or vomited to control your weight? ☐

If you scored 15 points and above, you may have an eating disorder. Please talk with a friend, family member, or school professional about a possible problem.

OVERCOMING SUBSTANCE ABUSE

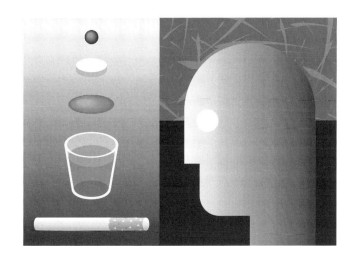

Overcoming Substance Abuse

This chapter includes information about nicotine, alcohol, and drug abuse awareness. There is a section that focuses on children of alcoholic or drug-abusing parents. Awareness, prevention, and coping are the key components of this section. The activity sheets help evaluate whether someone may have a problem with any of these substances and offers coping skills and ways to get help.

Time Allotment

Two 50-minute sessions integrated into a series of 50-minute class periods.

Goals

To provide comprehensive information about nicotine, alcohol, and drugs. To learn alternative coping skills for dealing with these addictions as well as for living in a family where someone has an addiction.

Objectives

- A student will become familiar with the statistics and facts on nicotine, alcohol, and drugs.
- A student will be able to identify at least five coping skills dealing with these addictions.
- A student will be able to verbalize five destructive patterns that children of addicts use to cope with their situation.

NICOTINE: DEADLY ADDICTION

Cigarette smoking has been called the "chief, single, avoidable cause of death in our society and the most important public health issue of our time." Smoking reduces the rate of lung growth in adolescents and lowers fitness levels. It causes shortness of breath, wheezing, and overall diminished health. It discolors your teeth, gives you really bad breath, and makes your clothes smell.

It also results in nicotine addiction, a condition that is extremely difficult to reverse. Most kids know this. They've seen relatives with lung cancer and may know people who have died from diseases caused by nicotine addiction. They see people so desperate to smoke that they will go outside in bad weather to do so. They think this is ridiculous, even pathetic. So why do they start smoking themselves?

Kids think that because they are young and in the prime of life, they are immune to the bad effects of smoking. They think the "Cigarettes are hazardous to your health" warnings don't apply to them. But this simply isn't true. Other myths include:

Myth: *Smoking relieves stress.*
Truth: *Smoking does not relieve anything.* It's simply something to do with your hands. When you feel stress, it may become second nature to reach for a cigarette but smoking will not reduce your anxiety. You soon become dependent on cigarettes and find you can't tackle non-stressful events without a cigarette. Your dependency actually creates stress, because you're always trying to figure out when and where you can smoke.

Myth: *Smoking helps you lose weight.*
Truth: *Weight loss and gain are caused by what you eat more than smoking.* Some smokers lose weight, some gain. Smoking increases your need to keep your mouth busy, so it can actually increase your desire to eat. When you smoke, you don't feel much like exercising, and inactivity is a factor in weight gain.

Myth: *Smoking helps you fit in.*
Truth: *If you're smoking because your friends smoke, you're not thinking for yourself.* If you feel you must smoke to fit in, then maybe you're in the wrong group. If you're trying to impress people, think again—a lot of people think smoking is gross and disgusting.

When you feel stress, it may become second nature to reach for a cigarette but smoking will not reduce your anxiety.

NICOTINE FACTS

Nicotine, the substance in cigarettes that causes craving and eventual addiction, is a drug as harmful as any other. Smoking kills an estimated 434,000 Americans each year—one person every 10 seconds—most of whom began smoking during adolescence. Consider these facts:

- Tobacco kills three times more people than alcohol, AIDS, drugs, car accidents, and murder and suicide combined.

- More than 3,000 American teens become regular smokers each day, with girls smoking at a higher rate than boys.

- American teens spend more than $1 billion a year on tobacco.

- The average smoker spends $500 to $700 a year on cigarettes. With $500 you could go to 83 movies, rent 125 videos, buy a racing bike, go to 12 concerts, or buy a plane ticket.

- Ninety percent of smokers begin before age 21, and 60 percent before age 14. The younger people are when they start to smoke, the more likely they are to become strongly addicted to nicotine.

- By age 18, one in three persons are using tobacco.

- If you don't start smoking as a teenager, you are unlikely ever to become a smoker.

- Teens who smoke cigarettes are 3 times more likely to use alcohol, 8 times more likely to use marijuana, and 22 times more likely to go on to cocaine than those who don't.

- Children from families in which one or both parents smoke are twice as likely to smoke as kids whose parents don't smoke.

- Every cigarette you smoke takes seven minutes off your life.

- Nearly two-thirds of smokers say they would like to quit. Seven of ten teen smokers regret ever starting. Three of four have tried to quit at least once and failed.

- Children whose parents smoke have a greater risk of disease including asthma, pneumonia, and bronchitis.

- Cancer death rates in cigar smokers are 34 percent higher than in non-smokers.

- Chewing tobacco is also bad for you. It discolors teeth, damages gums, and causes mouth and throat cancers.

American teens spend more than $1 billion a year on tobacco.

Seven of ten teen smokers regret ever starting. Three of four have tried to quit at least once and failed.

SAYING NO TO SMOKING

Saying "no" may well be the right thing to do, but it is much harder than just going along with the crowd. When everyone else wants you to join them, it's up to you to be strong enough to refuse. Consider these tips:

- **Even if you're curious, don't try it.** At some point, most kids wonder what it's like to smoke, especially when others are telling them that it feels great or that it's a rush. But what really happens is your throat and lungs burn, you cough, you feel sick, your eyes water, your heart speeds up, and it's hard to breathe.

- **Find friends who don't smoke.** This is hard to do, especially when you've made friends with people who do smoke. But it will be worth it— if your friends don't smoke, it's likely that you won't either. If your parents smoke, it's up to you to choose not to.

- **Just say "no."** This seems like a cliché, but you have to be ready to say it, instead of being wishy-washy. If you say, "No thanks, I don't smoke," people who matter to you will be more likely to respect you.

- **Don't fall for Joe Camel.** Teens are the largest population group targeted by tobacco companies. Cartoon characters and other incentives are designed to make smoking look fun, sexy, and cool. But it's none of those things. These companies are going after your money—and your health. Remember this: Two Marlboro Men died from lung cancer, and Joe Camel can smoke all he wants—he's a cartoon.

- **Stay busy.** Keeping busy will keep your mind occupied, and you won't think about smoking. Join a team or after-school club, or find a hobby you enjoy. At parties, keep your hands and mouth busy by talking, eating, and so on.

- **Be proud of yourself.** Never feel insecure or guilty about your choice not to smoke. Give yourself some strokes for staying away from this deadly habit.

If you already smoke and want to quit, here are some pointers:

- Join a program.
- Choose a specific day to quit so you won't procrastinate, and tell others what day it is.
- Learn about withdrawal symptoms and expect them.
- Take it step by step instead of cold turkey.
- Keep busy and active.
- Get support from friends and family.
- Stay away from other smokers.

Never feel insecure or guilty about your choice not to smoke.

THE FACTS ON ALCOHOL ABUSE

Alcohol is the No. 1 killer of teenagers. It makes you high while you're drinking, but afterward its depressant qualities make you feel worse. It has many negative effects on the body: It changes the way your mind works, interferes with good judgment, slows muscle control and reaction time, alters vision, and gives you the feeling that you are more in control than usual.

Alcohol use leaves you vulnerable to accidents, has a bad effect on your schoolwork, and can cause you to make unsafe decisions about sex.

The false sense of reality that alcohol induces can lead to disastrous results. Consider these facts:

- Alcohol is the drug teens tend to use first, at the earliest age. The average age of first use is 14, although it can be before age 12. The average grade for first use is 9th grade; however, 56 percent of high school seniors have reported initial use before high school.

- There are an estimated 3 million adolescent alcoholics in the United States.

- Six out of 10 kids have tried alcohol by the time they are in 9th grade, and 40 percent have gotten drunk.

- Eight thousand young people die each year in car accidents that involve alcohol use.

- Alcohol is involved in most violent deaths suffered by teens, and its use is closely linked to teen suicide.

- According to the FBI, alcohol is involved in 66 percent of all fatal accidents, 70 percent of all murders, 41 percent of all assaults, 53 percent of all fire deaths, 50 percent of all rapes, 60 percent of all crimes against children, 60 percent of all child abuse, 56 percent of all fights and assaults in the home, 37 percent of all suicides, and 55 percent of all arrests.

- Students with grades of D and F drink three times as much as those who earn As.

- Teens who drink alcohol are 50 times more likely to use cocaine than those who don't.

- Teens who have a high tolerance for alcohol are more likely to become alcoholics than those who get drunk easily.

- Teens who are addicted to alcohol before age 18 have only a 50 percent chance of living until they reach their 30th birthday.

Alcohol is involved in most violent deaths suffered by teens, and its use is closely linked to teen suicide.

Teens who are addicted to alcohol before age 18 have only a 50 percent chance of living until they reach their 30th birthday.

ALCOHOL MYTHS AND TRUTHS

People who drink spend a lot of time convincing themselves that there's nothing wrong with their behavior. Here are some of the myths:

Myth: *Alcohol makes me feel better.*
Truth: Drinking may numb painful feelings, but it doesn't make the feelings go away. The "good" feeling is temporary. Afterward you actually feel worse, especially if you're depressed.

Myth: *I'm more interesting when I'm drunk.*
Truth: Ask anyone who's been sober at a party where everyone else is drinking, and he/she will tell you you're wrong. People who are drunk laugh at things that aren't funny and talk about superficial things. There's a false sense of fun and security that dissipates as soon as people stop drinking.

Myth: *I can handle my drinking.*
Truth: Because your body is still growing, the negative effects of alcohol can hit you much faster than they affect an adult. Alcohol can also exaggerate "normal" depression, and even play a part in suicide.

Myth: *Binge drinking isn't dangerous.*
Truth: When you drink a lot of alcohol in a very short time, you end up getting drunk faster. You quickly lose control of your body and mind. Many adolescents die each year from alcohol poisoning. This happens when the body is unable to process the alcohol and clear it from the system.

Myth: *Everybody does it.*
Truth: Not everybody does it. A recent survey determined that 50 percent to 75 percent of adolescent girls do not drink. You do not have to drink to fit in and make friends.

Myth: *Alcohol is safer than drugs.*
Truth: Alcohol is involved in most violent deaths suffered by teens and its use is closely linked to teen suicide. The death toll for teens who drink is higher than for those who abuse drugs.

Myth: *Drinking makes sex more fun.*
Truth: Alcohol usually impairs sexual functioning. It also hinders your ability to make safe choices about sex.

Myth: *Wine coolers and beer are safer than hard liquor.*
Truth: These contain the same drug that liquor contains—alcohol. Alcohol in any form is harmful.

Myth:
One drink won't hurt.
Truth:
One drink
leads to another.
The more you drink,
the less able you are
to know when to stop.

Myth:
I can handle
my alcohol consumption.
Truth:
Being able to drink more
isn't a sign of strength.
It's an indication
of increased tolerance,
a sign of addiction.

THE FACTS ON DRUG ABUSE

Teens abuse a variety of drugs, both legal and illegal. Legally available drugs include alcohol, prescribed medications, inhalants (fumes from glues, aerosols, and solvents), and over-the-counter cough, cold, sleep, and diet medications. The most commonly used illegal drugs are marijuana (pot), stimulants (cocaine, crack, and speed), LSD, PCP, opiates, heroin, and designer drugs (Ecstasy).

Once you are addicted to drugs, you no longer have control over your life. You no longer care about friends, family, school, or basic things such as eating, sleeping, and generally taking care of yourself. Your urge to get high becomes more important than anything else. The only thing that will make the urge go away is to get high. Nothing else matters.

Teens who think the risks from using drugs are minimal are those who will use them. But drug use leads to drug addiction, and the seriousness of drug addiction can't be overstated. Here are some alarming facts:

- Children who are addicted to drugs before age 18 have only a 50 percent chance of living until they reach their 30th birthday.

- Teens who are at risk for developing serious drug problems are those with a family history of substance abuse, who are depressed, who have low self-esteem, and who feel they don't fit in.

- The tar and chemicals in marijuana have been shown to be as damaging to human lungs as the nicotine in cigarettes.

- Frequent cocaine use can lead to nasal and breathing problems, paranoia, and even death from cardiac arrest, respiratory failure, and brain hemorrhage.

- The average age of first marijuana use is 14. By the time they are in 9th grade, one out of four adolescents has used drugs. More than half of high school students have used drugs.

- A recent poll found that adolescents listed drugs as the most important problem facing people their age, followed by crime and violence in school and social pressures.

- Another study indicated that one-half of juniors and seniors said it would be easy to buy drugs while at school.

Once you are addicted to drugs, you no longer have control over your life.

SAYING NO TO ALCOHOL AND DRUGS

It's hard to say no. When a friend asks you to join him, all kinds of thoughts go through your mind. Should I do it? Will he still like me if I don't? What'll happen if I do? What'll happen if I don't? Here are ten tips for saying no:

1. Plan ahead. If you're invited to a party, think ahead about the situation. Will alcohol and drugs be available? Will the parents be home? Are you going with friends who can say no? Will you have to ride with someone who may get drunk or high? Can you call one of your parents or another adult if you want to leave?

2. Have an exit plan. If the party gets too rowdy, or if you feel that you're in an unsafe situation, you may want or need to leave. What if a friend goes off and leaves you and you don't want to stay? Can someone pick you up? Do you have money for a taxi?

3. If you don't want to go, don't go. If you know ahead of time that you may be in an uncomfortable position, call another friend and make another plan.

4. Focus on other activities. If you pursue a hobby or a sport, the things you do in your free time can revolve around these activities. When you're busy doing something you like, you won't have time to drink and use drugs.

5. Be yourself. Many teens feel that there's safety in numbers—that being like everyone else is the best course of action. But if you learn to think and do things independently of everyone else, your self-esteem will improve, and you'll think twice when someone offers you a drink or drugs.

6. Choose friends wisely. Think about what you want in a friend. Is it important to have a group of friends? If it is, it's likely that you'll do what everyone else is doing, and that might mean drinking and using drugs. If you feel that your friendships are stronger than this, you should be able to decide together that you'll help each other when alcohol and drugs enter the picture.

7. Practice saying no. "Thanks, I already have something to drink" is a good way to refuse alcohol, but saying "I don't drink" or "I don't do drugs" is more effective. Either way, you get your message across. It's hard to refuse, but if you practice, it will get easier and feel more natural.

8. Be supportive. Help others say no, and help them get away from drugs and drinking. Make a pact with your friends to help each other at parties and other situations where you might be tempted.

(continued)

If you're drinking to relieve sadness or stress, alcohol can make you feel worse. Drugs may give you a brief high, but the high always ends, and your feelings are still there.

(continued)

9. Face your feelings. When you use alcohol and drugs, it's usually a sign that something else is wrong. If you're drinking to relieve sadness or stress, alcohol can make you feel worse. Drugs may give you a brief high, but the high always ends, and your feelings are still there.

10. Reach out. Realize that you're not alone if you feel you have an alcohol or drug problem. Make an effort to get to know people who don't drink or use drugs, or reach out to an adult for help.

CHILDREN OF ALCOHOLICS AND DRUG ABUSERS

Children of parents who abuse drugs or alcohol are at the highest risk of developing addictions themselves or marrying someone who may develop an addiction.

But do you want to have the kind of life your parent has? Has he/she been the kind of parent you hope to be someday? You have the choice to become like your parent, or to work hard to be different.

You're not alone. Consider this: There are 28 million children of alcohol- and drug-abusing parents in the United States, or one in every four children. Close to half of these children have emotional and health problems and are likely to become alcohol or drug abusers themselves.

Children of such parents are constantly subjected to inconsistent behavior by the chemical-abusing parent. In order to cope, these children commonly:

- Deny that the alcohol dependence exists.
- Minimize the importance of the chemical dependence.
- Repress any memory of the chemical dependence.
- Feel that the chemical dependence is their fault.
- Feel anxious and worry about the family's problems.
- Feel embarrassed about their situation at home.
- Feel confused, scared, and uncertain due to the drinking parent's mood swings and unpredictable behavior.
- Feel anger and resentment at both the drinking parent and the non-drinking parent for lack of support and protection.
- Feel depressed, lonely, and helpless.

Teens who are sexually or physically abused, live in a violent family, or don't have a caring adult in their lives are also more likely to abuse alcohol and other drugs.

If you're worried about a parent's drinking or you need to talk to people who understand what you're experiencing, you can call Alateen, a support group for teens with alcoholic parents. The number is listed in your phone book.

There are 28 million children of alcohol- and drug-abusing parents in the United States, or one in every four children.

ACTIVITY: TROUBLE SIGNS

If you or a friend is in trouble with alcohol or drug use, it's never too late to get help and turn things around. Here's a checklist of possible trouble signs. If you check yes for four or more of these statements, it's time to talk to someone about getting help.

	YES	NO
Do you hang out with people who drink or use drugs?	☐	☐
Have you been getting in trouble at school?	☐	☐
Have your grades lowered significantly?	☐	☐
Have you stopped caring about your appearance?	☐	☐
Have you been avoiding going home or to school?	☐	☐
Have you lost interest in things you used to like to do?	☐	☐
Do you use alcohol or drugs to solve your problems?	☐	☐
Have you been drinking or using drugs to relieve stress?	☐	☐
Do you always think about the next time you'll drink?	☐	☐
Do you always think about the next time you'll use drugs?	☐	☐
Is your speech slurred?	☐	☐
Do you feel tired all the time?	☐	☐
Do you lie, cheat, steal, or borrow money a lot?	☐	☐
Are you drinking or using drugs alone?	☐	☐
Do you have blackouts?	☐	☐
Are your parents suspicious of your behavior?	☐	☐
Do you fight with your parents a lot?	☐	☐
Do your siblings see you get drunk or high?	☐	☐
Do you offer alcohol or drugs to your siblings?	☐	☐
Do you drink quickly to get drunk?	☐	☐
Do you use drugs to get high quickly?	☐	☐
Does your personality change when you're drinking?	☐	☐
Does your personality change when you're using drugs?	☐	☐
Do you think you can do anything when high or drunk?	☐	☐
Do you drive while high or drunk?	☐	☐
Do your friends like you better when you're high/drunk?	☐	☐
Do you like your friends better when you're high/drunk?	☐	☐
Do you have little or no control over how drunk you get?	☐	☐
Do you have little or no control over how high you get?	☐	☐
Do you need to use drugs or drink?	☐	☐
Do you think you could stop cold turkey?	☐	☐
Have you been trying to stop but can't?	☐	☐

Getting and giving help are not easy, but they are key to being able to stop drinking or using drugs.

Complete this exercise:

I've decided to stop drinking/using drugs because _____
_____ .

When I tell my friends that I've decided to stop drinking/using drugs, this is what I'll say: _____
_____ .

When I stop, I'll try to get more friendly with: _____
and _____ because they don't use drugs.
I'll also ask my family to help me. This is what I'll say: _____
_____ .

When I want to go to a party where there may be drugs and/or alcohol, this is what I'll tell myself or do: _____
_____ .

If I get stuck in a place where there's drugs and/or alcohol, this is what I'll do: _____
_____ .

Having an addiction doesn't mean I'm a bad person, because _____
_____ .

Complete this exercise if you are going to help a friend stop:

I'm going to help (name of friend) stop drinking/using drugs. I'll be supportive by _____
_____ .

If he/she calls me for help, I'll tell him/her _____
_____ .

If he/she backslides a little, I'll _____
_____ .

Some activities we can do together that don't involve alcohol or drugs are _____
_____ .

I'll encourage him/her by saying _____
_____ .

SUICIDE ASSESSMENT AND INTERVENTION

Suicide Assessment and Intervention

This chapter describes why some children commit suicide and lists the signs and behaviors that could indicate when someone is at risk for committing suicide. It states vital but disturbing facts and statistics on this issue and offers coping skills to help children or their friends if there is indication of suicidal thoughts, feelings, or behaviors.

Time Allotment

Two 50-minute sessions integrated into a series of 50-minute class periods.

Goal

To understand why someone may commit suicide and the reasons behind this devastating event. To learn the warning signs that indicate when someone may want to harm herself and to provide alternative methods of coping with loss, depression, abandonment, family issues, etc.

Objectives

- A student will become familiar with the statistics on suicide.
- A student will be able to identify at least five reasons why someone may want to harm himself or herself.
- A student will be able to verbalize five warning signs of suicide.
- A student will be able to list five out of ten feelings expressed that might indicate suicidal behavior.

WHY DO CHILDREN COMMIT SUICIDE?

As hard as it may be to comprehend, it's reported that every 90 minutes a child or adolescent commits suicide. For 15- to 24-year-olds, suicide is the third-leading cause of death in the United States after accidents and homicide. What makes these children so unhappy that they feel that death is the only way out? And how are the people they leave behind—family members, friends, and the community at large—supposed to cope with and understand such a final, desperate act?

Adolescents who attempt or commit suicide often have a background of frustration and conflict with the important people in their lives. Most children who are both depressed and suicidal are reacting to some type of loss, either of an object, person, or state of well being.

Children may also consider suicide because of family problems and conflicts, pressures of sexual relationships, sexual abuse, homosexuality, unwanted pregnancy, a feeling of being unable to fit in, a history of substance abuse, or the pain of dealing with an eating disorder.

Other considerations in suicidal thinking include the sense of loss a child feels as a result of divorce, a move to another place, a breakup with a boyfriend or girlfriend, failing an exam, or not making a sports team. These losses are accompanied by low self-esteem and feelings of helplessness. Suicidal children feel that they can't talk to anyone about their feelings. They think no one understands, and because they are so sad, they can't see any other way to end the pain. Unfortunately, they often don't comprehend that suicide is always final; there's no turning back.

For every child or teenager who actually commits suicide, many more seriously consider it or make some kind of attempt, putting them at risk in the future to commit suicide. Suicidal teenagers usually talk about suicide before their death, but this often happens so close to the actual suicide that others don't realize that it's about to happen. Most leave suicide notes, which reflect intense anger and feelings of worthlessness. Once a child has tried to commit suicide and failed, if he doesn't get professional help he will probably try again, and this time he may be successful.

What makes these children so unhappy that they feel that death is the only way out?

SUICIDE STATISTICS

- Suicide is the third-leading cause of death of adolescents, preceded only by homicide and accidents.

- Children and adolescents who are most at risk for suicide include those who abuse drugs, live in an unstable home environment, have eating disorders, move a lot, were sexually and/or physically abused as children, have been arrested, are gay, have a history of running away from home, and have failed a grade.

- The incidence of suicide among 15- to 19-year-old males increased from just under 6 per 100,000 in 1965 to 17.8 per 100,000 in 1992.

- According to a recent survey, between 6 percent and 13 percent of all adolescents reported that they attempted suicide at least once in their lives, compared with a reported 1 percent in 1960.

- It is estimated that there are 100 to 120 suicide attempts for every suicide.

- More than 40 percent of adolescents who suicide have made previous attempts, and 3 percent to 10 percent do so within 15 years of their first attempt.

- Each year between 7,000 and 12,000 children in the United States have a parent who commits suicide.

- It has been estimated that a suicide results in a 300 percent increase in the likelihood that others at the deceased's school will commit suicide.

- Twenty-five thousand children are hospitalized annually in the United States because they express suicidal thoughts.

- A suicide attempt is not usually an impulsive act. Investigations show that suicidal children think about the idea frequently and perhaps even plan for it for a long time.

- If a family history of suicide exists, the odds become greater that a child in that family will attempt suicide.

SIGNS OF SUICIDAL FEELINGS

• **Crying out for help.** A child may make a desperate attempt to relieve overwhelming feelings of frustration and confusion over family conflicts or life events with repeated statements: "I can't go on. I don't see a way out. It's hopeless."

• **Self-anger and self-hatred.** These may reflect angry feelings that can't be expressed toward others. A typical statement: "I hate myself. I don't deserve to live. I deserve to die."

• **Flirting with death.** When children and teens play dangerous games they're often trying to get their peers to think they're cool. A typical dare: "I dare you to drag race at 100 miles per hour."

• **Losing touch with reality.** Suicidal children and adolescents can become so disoriented that they can no longer distinguish between fact and fiction. A typical statement: "I'm going to jump off this building and fly."

• **Being preoccupied with death.** Children at risk to commit suicide often become obsessed with death and dying. There will be a preoccupation with themes of death or dying in artwork, movies, videos, and songs. Suicidal teenagers sometimes plan their own funerals or give away their cherished belongings. A typical statement: "I'd like roses at my funeral. I'm giving all of my jewelry to Pam."

• **Becoming socially isolated.** As thoughts of suicide and feelings of depression increase, socialization decreases. A typical statement: "I have no friends. No one likes me or wants to be with me. What's the use?"

• **Prolonged grief.** A child may mourn the loss of a loved one (family member or friend) for an extended period of time. A typical statement: "I wish I was dead, too."

• **Wishing to punish or get even**. An adolescent suffering a loss may make threats to deal with anger toward the person who has died. A typical statement: "Dad will be sorry he ever punished me. I'll show him."

• **Attempting to regain power or control.** Children suffering from a loss often feel helpless and struggle for control. A typical statement: "You can't leave me; I'm leaving you."

• **Wishing to die to relieve tremendous guilt.** Suicidal children and adolescents may blame themselves wrongly. A typical statement: "I can't forgive myself for Mom's death. I know I caused it. I was so mean to her the night before she died, so I'm going to die too."

As thoughts of suicide and feelings of depression increase, socialization decreases.

In order to understand why children attempt and commit suicide—and to prevent it—it's important to realize that some of the common perceptions are myths. They just aren't true. Here are some common ones:

• **Most people who commit suicide are crazy.** Most people are not "crazy," in that they are able to lead apparently normal, even successful lives until the moment they decide to kill themselves.

• **People who talk about suicide never follow through.** People, even children, who talk of suicide, do kill themselves. Statements about suicide, of not wanting to go on anymore, of despair, and of hopelessness are cries for help.

• **Children under the age of six do not commit suicide.** Evidence has shown that five-, four-, and even three-year-olds have been clearly suicidal. Abused children often regard themselves with the same hostility and criticism as their parents do, forming a bad self-image that can lead to suicide.

• **Children are incapable of implementing a suicide plan.** Children who contemplate, threaten, or attempt suicide in the six- to 12-year-old group most frequently use jumping from heights, ingesting poison, hanging, stabbing, drowning, running into traffic, and burning. Television often provides the model, means, and method. None of these methods requires any lengthy or complicated planning or specific physical attainment.

• **Suicidal children are fully intent on dying.** There is an ambivalence about dying. Children need to end the pain, but there is always the wish that something or someone will remove the pain so life can continue.

• **When the mood of the depressed child changes, the crisis is over.** When a child's mood or behavior gets better, it may be because indecision concerning suicide is over. A decision has been made and the anxiety is past, but that decision could be for suicide.

• **Talking about suicide puts forbidden thoughts into a suicidal child's head.** A suicidal child already has such thoughts. Talking about suicide removes a child's fears that he is crazy and alone, takes away the guilt for thinking that way, and opens avenues for resolution of suicidal thoughts.

• **Once children contemplate or attempt suicide, they should be considered suicidal for the rest of their lives.** When the crisis is over and the problems leading to suicidal thoughts are resolved, suicidal thoughts usually end. It's possible, however, that suicide will still be an option for another time, if things become bad again.

When a child's mood or behavior gets better, it may be because indecision concerning suicide is over.

SUICIDE WARNING SIGNS

If you suspect a friend is suicidal, look for the warning signs listed below. They are pretty good indicators that something is seriously wrong. It is estimated that at least 75 percent of kids who commit suicide exhibit a series of common behaviors. If you think a friend or classmate is suicidal, tell an adult. It doesn't matter if you're wrong—take the risk; next time you may be right. If you know what to look for, you could save a life.

- Hurting oneself on purpose.
- Personality changes or significant changes in behavior.
- Changes in eating patterns such as loss of appetite or excessive overeating.
- Changes in sleeping patterns, such as insomnia or oversleeping, lasting for several days.
- Not wanting to participate in favorite activities.
- Breaking off completely from important relationships.
- Expressed feelings of hopelessness, helplessness, anxiety, guilt, and/or difficulty concentrating.
- Suicidal thoughts, ideas, threats, or plans, especially if the plan is specific or lethal.
- Verbal comments such as plans to "end it all" or "I can't take it any more."
- Declarations such as "I'm going away on a long trip," "You won't have to worry about me anymore," "I just want to sleep and never wake up."
- Preoccupation with death or suicide, or similar themes in movies, songs, artwork, etc.
- An increase in self-destructive behavior and excessive risk-taking.
- A change from depression to lightheartedness, sudden elation, or a sudden switch away from talking about suicide.
- Making a will and/or giving away prized possessions: pictures, clothes, CDs, etc.
- Unusual neglect of appearance, self-deprecation, and/or self-destructive behavior.

There are many ways to help a suicidal friend. Most importantly, any suggestion of suicide must be taken seriously. This can't be stressed enough—if you help a person who is suicidal, you can save his life. Here are some things to remember:

• **People who talk about suicide are the ones who commit suicide.** Of course, some don't, but many do. It's been found that more than 75 percent of all completed suicides did things prior to their deaths to try to show others that they were in emotional pain. If you suspect a friend is suicidal, tell an adult.

• **Something that seems trivial to you may be unbearable to someone else.** People commit suicide because they are hurting. Don't dismiss that hurt because it seems trivial to you.

• **Suicidal behavior is a cry for help.** Most suicidal people want to remain alive. They don't really want to end their lives. They just want their lives to be better, for their pain to end. The part of a person that tells another person "I feel like I want to kill myself" is also the part that is saying "I want to live."

• **Don't wait to get help or to find out how to help.** You should know what to do in such a situation beforehand. By the time a person is ready to end his life, he has been thinking about it for a long time, and he probably hasn't sought help before. So timing is critical. If you wait, it may be too late.

• **Talk with the person about how he is planning to do it.** Talking about suicide won't plant the idea. It's already there, loud and clear. As you listen to the person, he will perceive that you care about him and want to hear what he has to say. For the time being, he may decide against it.

• **Don't leave the person alone.** If he is about to kill himself, try to divert him in any way you can. Try to get rid of weapons and/or drugs. Assure him that he has done the right thing by notifying you, and send someone to get help or call 911.

• **Don't keep it a secret.** It's important for others to know what happened. They will help you get help. This is not a situation that should be considered secret or embarrassing. Others can learn from it.

Talking about suicide won't plant the idea. It's already there, loud and clear

HANDLING A CALL FROM A SUICIDAL PERSON

You may find yourself in a situation where helping a person who is serious about suicide is crucial but you're not there with him. Here is some helpful advice:

• **Try to be yourself.** Your voice and manner will reflect that you are upset, and that is okay. The "right" words are not important at this stage.

• **Listen.** Let the person talk to you. Try not to intervene too much. No matter how bleak the situation may seem, the fact that the person called you is a good sign—a cry for help.

• **Sympathize and be understanding.** Don't give assurances that "everything will be okay." Be calm, patient, and non-judgmental. Avoid arguments and advice. Simply tell the person that you're glad he called you.

• **Ask, "Are you having thoughts of suicide?"** If the person says something like "I'm so depressed; I can't go on," it's okay to ask this question. You're not giving him the idea of suicide; rather, you're showing him that you care, that you're taking him seriously, and that it's okay for him to share his pain with you.

• **Get specifics.** If the person is considering suicide, ask: (1) Have you thought about how you'd do it? (2) Do you have what you need to do it? and (3) Have you thought about when you'd do it? Research has shown that 95 percent of all suicidal callers will answer "no" to at least one of these questions, or will say that they're going to do it "sometime in the future."

• **Recognize that the call is a cry for help.** Simply talking about the pain brings some relief. It shows the person that someone cares.

• **If the person has taken an overdose of drugs, get the details.** Find out the name of the drug, how much he took, whether any alcohol or other medications are involved, and when he had his last meal. Get someone else to call the local Poison Control Center while you continue to talk to the person, or ask the person to listen in while you make the call on another phone. If you need immediate assistance, call an ambulance, or ask the person if a nearby neighbor, relative, or friend can be contacted for transportation.

• **Try to get help for yourself during the call.** You need support, too. Tell someone what happened immediately afterward.

• **Offer to get professional help.** The most important resource for a suicidal person is a trained mental health professional.

No matter how bleak the situation may seem, the fact that the person called you is a good sign — a cry for help.

You will not feel relief if you are dead.

. . . it's a good thing you're reading this page. It may mean that you're still unsure about killing yourself, and that you're looking for help. Even though you may be feeling intense pain, you're still unsure about ending your life.

The end of life is just that—it's final. Keep these important things to keep in mind:

• **You are not a bad, crazy, or weak person because you are having suicidal thoughts.** You're just a person who has too much to deal with, and you need help. Your pain may not seem too bad to another person, but that doesn't matter—you're the one who has to deal with it. If your coping mechanisms aren't strong enough, you can get help to make them stronger.

• **People do get through this, even those who are feeling as badly as you are now.** Statistically, there's a good chance that you are not going to commit suicide.

• **Give yourself 24 hours before you do anything.** Just because you feel like killing yourself doesn't mean that you have to do it right now.

• **People often turn to suicide because they are seeking relief from pain.** However, to feel relief, you have to be alive. You will not feel relief if you are dead.

• **Realize that some people will react badly to your suicidal feelings.** They may do or say thoughtless things to you because they are frightened or angry. They are not angry with you, but they are terrified by how they would feel if you actually did kill yourself: scared, angry, and, above all, grief-stricken.

• **There are people who can spend time with you and help you.** They won't judge you, or argue with you, or try to tell you everything will be okay. They will simply care for you and listen to you. A suicide hotline, a therapist, or a clergyperson are places and people to call for help. Just talking about how you feel can help for the time being and that may be enough time for you to regain your balance and go on with life.

Imagine yourself having to deal with a suicidal friend. Here are some situations and statements. Next to each, write what you'd say to help your friend through the crisis.

• Your friend is really angry and hurting about his parents' divorce. He's thinking of killing himself, and says, "They'll be sorry now!"

What would you say? _____

_____

• Your friend is suicidal because he's convinced that nobody in his family cares whether he lives or dies. He's decided to leave a suicide note telling family members exactly what he wants them to do when he's gone. He says, "They won't be able to ignore me now!"

What would you say? _____

_____

• Your friend has a fantasy that he'll be considered a saint at his own funeral. He's sure he'll be there to witness it, and says, "Everyone will come to my funeral, and they'll all love me then!"

What would you say? _____

_____

• Your friend is still grieving for her mother who died recently. She's angry with her mother for leaving her, but she thinks that if she can be with her again, everything will be all right. She's thinking of committing suicide because, as she says, "I can be with my mom."

What would you say? _____

_____

• Your friend is so depressed that he can't stand living anymore. He tells you, "I just want to put an end to the pain."

What would you say? _____

_____

ACTIVITY: ARE YOU AT RISK FOR SUICIDE?

There are certain conditions and emotional changes that are associated with suicide risk. If you think you may be suicidal, check the situations or changes that have occurred in your life to see if you are at risk. If you check four or more, talk to a mental health professional or other trusted adult.

☐ The death or terminal illness of a loved one

☐ Your parents' divorce or separation

☐ Your loss of health (mental or physical)

☐ Your parents' loss of job, home, or financial status

☐ Alcohol and/or drug abuse in your family

☐ Depression

☐ Overwhelming, all-encompassing emotional pain

☐ Hopelessness: the feeling that things will never get better

☐ Helplessness: the feeling that you can't help yourself

☐ Worthlessness, shame, self-hatred

☐ Pervasive sadness, tiredness, anxiety, and/or irritability

☐ Decline in school performance

☐ A complete break-off from your friends

☐ Disinterest in things you used to enjoy doing

☐ Neglect of personal appearance and hygiene

☐ Difference in sleeping habits

☐ Difference in eating habits

☐ Difficulty at holiday time or on birthdays

☐ Previous suicide attempts

☐ Statements about suicide

☐ Self-inflicted injuries

☐ Reckless behavior; putting yourself and others in danger

☐ Verbal statements that suggest suicide

GRIEF AND LOSS

Grief and Loss

Dealing with grief and loss can be especially devastating for children and adolescents. This chapter reviews the stages of grief and the factors that influence how children react when they lose someone or something. It describes various levels of grief, specifically focusing on the death of a sibling, complicated grief, death of a pet, and dealing with holidays. Coping skills are woven throughout the chapter in an attempt to provide a comprehensive look at ways to deal with grief and loss with children. The activity handouts focus on helping students learn to express their feelings.

Time Allotment

Two 50-minute sessions integrated into a series of 50-minute class periods.

Goal

To help students learn coping skills to deal with grief and loss.

Objectives

- A student will be able to list the five stages of grief.
- A student will become familiar with several factors that influence how someone deals with grief and loss.
- A student will learn three to four coping skills for different types of grief and loss.

THE STAGES OF GRIEF

Death is a natural part of life. Sooner or later, everyone experiences the death of a loved one, friend, acquaintance, or pet. Still, it is never easy to deal with death. Death requires us to go on without someone we know or love when it seems almost impossible to do so.

There are five stages of grief:

Shock/denial/disbelief. This is the common reaction to news of a death. It may feel:
- As if you're on automatic pilot, like a robot.
- Numbing—you may feel unable to cry although you feel you should.
- As if it's impossible that the world still exists as it did before.
- Strange that you can carry on as you did before.

Anger. There are many reasons for anger, and many people you may feel angry toward. You may be angry at:
- Your parent(s), for not telling you how sick the loved one was, for not taking better care of the loved one, or for being the surviving parent.
- Yourself, for not preventing the death, wishing the person would die, or not saying "good-bye" or "I love you."
- Your siblings, for not feeling as bad as you do or for not wanting to talk about the death.
- Your friends, for not caring enough, not saying the right things, or for not saying anything at all.
- The dead person, for putting him/herself in danger, for abandoning you, for committing suicide without considering your feelings, or for not fighting harder against death.

Bargaining. It's natural to feel responsible in some way for your loved one's death, even though you know intellectually that you're not. Here are some things you may think or say:
- "If I'd been there, I wouldn't have let him die."
- "It should have been me instead."
- "She died because I said 'I hate you.'"

Depression. A period of depression usually follows a major loss. You feel hopeless and helpless, as if the worst thing possible has happened. Depression can manifest itself in:
- Sleeping difficulties
- Restlessness
- Feelings of despair
- Poor concentration
- Eating too much or too little
- Lack of interest in school, friends, and life in general

It's natural to feel responsible in some way for your loved one's death.

A period of depression usually follows a major loss.

(continued)

(continued)

Acceptance/adjustment. Acceptance doesn't mean that you're "over" the death or that you've forgotten the dead person. It means that you've gone through the earlier stages of grief—you've expressed your anger, you've cried, and you've talked about your feelings—and now you've come to some sort of understanding of your loss. Your life has changed. You will always miss the loved one, and maybe you will feel sad off and on for a long time, but you've accepted the death and you're able to continue with your life.

GRIEF REACTIONS

We often experience feelings similar to the grief over a death when other events occur in our lives. A sibling may move away or go to college and you must readjust to life without him. Divorce brings about a grieving process as you adjust to life with one parent. The loss of innocence and control of your body that results from sexual abuse also involves grief. A breakup with a boyfriend or girlfriend is also a very real loss that causes grief.

Whatever you're feeling, it's a safe bet that the feelings are normal grief reactions. They may include:

• **Sadness.** Crying is a natural and necessary part of grief. It relieves the stress your body is feeling, and it can be very cleansing, giving you energy to go on. No one should ever tell you that you're too old to cry, or that you shouldn't cry for any other reason.

• **Guilt.** This is the feeling that is marked by "if only" and "should have": "If only I'd been nicer to him," "I should have said 'I love you.'" If you feel guilt, remember that arguments are a part of life, especially during adolescence. Also remember that you should never feel guilty about being angry, about what you did or didn't do.

• **Thoughts of suicide or homicide.** It's not unusual for children and adolescents to have thoughts of using suicide or homicide as a way of escaping their pain. If you have these thoughts, you must share them with someone who can help you with your despair.

• **Sexual activity.** Sometimes teens (and adults) become sexually active during a period of grief. If support is unavailable, the need to be physically close to someone is great. Sex fulfills this need, and it can be a distraction from pain. But the satisfaction it provides is temporary, as it often doesn't fulfill the emotional need that accompanies grief.

• **Drugs/alcohol.** It's a natural response to want to numb bad feelings. When you're drunk or high, you don't have to feel. Keep in mind that while alcohol and drugs may numb the pain, they also prolong and complicate the grieving process.

GRIEF AND TEENS

Teens experience the death of a loved one or friend much the same way as adults do, but because their ideas about the world and their self-identities are still being formed, they often have special concerns and unique feelings. These feelings are different from those they might have had as a child, and also different from those of adults.

If someone you love dies, you may feel inclined to turn into yourself and away from others. You may decide that you're never going to get close to anyone ever again, to avoid the hurt and pain you're feeling now. These feelings are real, and no one should ever deny them. Here are some of the factors that may affect the way you're feeling:

• **Teens are often told to "be strong."** Many adults think that because teens are no longer children, they should put on a "good face" and "carry on" for others. The truth is, however, that no one, not even an adult, should do this. Everyone, no matter his age, needs to go through the grieving process.

• **The death of a parent can be especially difficult for a teen.** When adolescents are busy separating from their parents, a parent's death can foster feelings of guilt and "unfinished business." Another issue involves the gap between your outward appearance and your inner feelings. You may look like an adult, but that may not mean you're emotionally mature enough to handle a devastating death.

• **Teens often experience sudden deaths.** Today's world is full of bad experiences, and your life may be touched by a parent's death due to illness, a friend's suicide, a sibling's car accident, or a school shooting. The negative effects of a sudden death may affect you for a very long time.

• **Support may not be there.** Because you may have been giving the message that you want to be on your own and make your own decisions, you may find that people are more than happy to leave you alone at a time when you are confused and in great pain. When a death occurs and the need for support is heightened, you may be expected to act "grown up" and support others. But it's extremely difficult to give support when you don't get it.

• **Your friends may act strangely for a while.** Support may not come from friends either: People who haven't experienced death may feel uncomfortable and ignore the subject entirely. It's up to you to find people with whom you can talk and express your feelings. And remember— no feeling or thought is too terrible to share.

Remember — no feeling or thought is too terrible to share.

COMPLICATED GRIEF

When children experience the traumatic death of a loved one, they may actually feel ashamed and embarrassed by it. The issues surrounding such deaths (for example, the anger and disbelief that surround a suicide, the stigma of an AIDS-related death, or the death of a sibling who was driving drunk) are complicated and confusing. The normal process of grieving becomes interrupted, and the feelings that accompany grief are denied and unexpressed. It's almost as though there's a wall between the grief and the child. Consider these examples:

• **Sudden or traumatic death due to murder, suicide, fatal accidents, or a sudden fatal illness creates an unstable environment in the home.** The surviving adults are trying to understand and deal with their own issues. Children are often left to fend for themselves when they most need attention.

• **Social stigma and shame frequently accompany deaths resulting from AIDS, suicide, and homicide.** People feel too embarrassed to talk honestly and openly about such issues. Children often don't want their peers to know how the loved one died. Their suppressed feelings are held in, becoming a form of self-hatred. They feel lonely and isolated and, most of all, ashamed.

• **Multiple losses can trigger a sense of fear or abandonment and self-doubt.** When a single parent dies, the child feels as if he has lost both parents, especially if the non-custodial parent lives far away. The child may have to live somewhere else, moving away from the rest of his family, friends, and familiar surroundings. This sudden and complete change of lifestyle can foster a strong fear of future abandonment.

• **If abuse, neglect, or abandonment is an issue, the death of the loved one can cause ambivalent feelings.** Part of the child feels relief, but he also feels embarrassed and ashamed by this feeling, even though the dead parent treated him so poorly. Guilt, fear, and depression often accompany this type of death.

• **If the surviving parent doesn't mourn, there's no role model for the child.** Feelings are denied and withheld. Or, if the parent is deeply involved in his own grief, the child may feel that he shouldn't burden the surviving parent with his issues and concerns. The child may become over-protective of the parent, fearing something may happen to that parent as well.

Social stigma and shame frequently accompany deaths resulting from AIDS, suicide, and homicide. People feel too embarrassed to talk honestly and openly about such issues.

Everyone needs to be allowed to grieve in his/her own time and way. It may take a long time —recovery doesn't follow a time schedule. If you are grieving, try these suggestions:

• **Don't hold in your feelings.** There is no right way to grieve. Whatever you're feeling, let it happen. Anger and tears are normal reactions whatever your age. Talk about your feelings with others.

• **Share a picture of the person who has died, and tell someone all about him.** Talk about why the person was special to you, but also talk about things you didn't like. Share whatever comes to mind.

• **Talk about your personal experience with the death**—where you were when it happened, what you thought and how you felt, and how you feel right now.

• **Write a letter to the dead person, and/or keep a journal.** This will allow you to say good-bye. It also provides a safe place for you to express your feelings. If you're angry, write about how you feel; if you're sad, write about that too.

• **Paint a portrait of the person who has died, or a make a collage as a tribute.** Collecting words, pictures, and other things that relate to the person and assembling them in one place can be a creative way of helping the healing process.

• **Allow yourself some simple pleasures.** These may be things you've never done before, such as taking a bubble bath, or going for a walk alone. Renting funny movies is also helpful.

• **Create some kind of ritual for the anniversary of the death.** Anniversaries can be especially difficult. Commemorating a death can be helpful, especially if you do something that was meaningful to the dead person or to you in relation to him/her.

• **Take care of your body.** The stress of loss will take a physical toll. Get enough sleep, eat well, and exercise.

• **Realize that the grief process will take you two steps forward and one step back.** You may feel okay one day and awful the next. Pain can be intense, but it won't always be constant. Don't feel guilty about feeling good; these moments will give you strength for the hard times.

• **Accept the death in your own way.** This doesn't mean forgetting—it means keeping your memories alive and letting the healing begin.

The stress of loss will take a physical toll. Get enough sleep, eat well, and exercise.

DEALING WITH HOLIDAYS

Holidays are not always filled with happy times and experiences. They can, in fact, be very stressful, especially for the people who have survived a loved one's death. Holiday customs and traditions are never quite the same and can seem empty and sad. Here are some suggestions for making holidays seem less stiff and strange:

• **Expect to feel sad.** When you and your family are facing a holiday or birthday without a loved one, you can expect it to be painful. Even though this is supposed to be a happy time, it's okay to be sad.

• **Don't try to ignore the holiday or special occasion.** The Christmas season, in particular, begins two months before the actual holiday. The reminders are everywhere, so ignoring them is almost impossible. Rather than trying to skip a holiday, think about how you'd like to celebrate it and discuss it with your family.

• **Don't pretend everything is okay or the same.** The death of your loved one has created a very real void in your life, and things will likely be very different at holiday time. It may help to remember that holidays are rarely as picture-perfect as the media tries to portray them.

• **Don't decide beforehand that everything will be terrible.** Dreading a holiday can make things worse. Chances are that once you get through it, you and your family will agree that it wasn't as bad as you expected.

• **Talk about the person who has died and how different things feel.** Holidays do not have to be "happy" times. They can be both happy and sad, bitter and sweet. Traditions can change, too, if rituals are too painful without the person who has died. If changes do occur, be flexible and try to realize that it's not always how things are done but the fact that they're done at all.

• **Make sure your parents acknowledge you and your special occasions.** They may have lost a loved one, but that doesn't give them permission to ignore you or other important parts of their life. Your birthday, in particular, is a very special occasion, designed to celebrate you. If you feel neglected, tell them.

Holidays do not have to be "happy" times. They can be both happy and sad, bitter and sweet.

THE DEATH OF A SIBLING

Each year more than 400,000 children under age 25 die from illness, suicide, murder, and accidents. The siblings who survive them number in the millions. Often these siblings feel sad, in pain, and guilty over the loss of a brother or sister.

If you've had such a loss, your family life will certainly change—things will never be the same as they were. Here are some things to remember:

• **You may feel guilty about your sibling's death.** This is a normal reaction. Your feelings stem from the years you spent as a brother or sister to your sibling, years that brought love and closeness, but also guilt, fear, resentment, rivalry for parental affection, hate, jealousy, anger, and other emotions.

• **You may be protected from family discussions about your sibling.** Even though you're old enough to be included, your parents may want to protect you. But it's better if your parents are honest with you, so that you can ask questions and get the answers you need.

Parents should know that you, the surviving sibling, need more love and attention than ever.

• **Your parents may neglect you as they sink deep into sorrow.** Parents should know that you, the surviving sibling, need more love and attention than ever. If they overlook you, let them know that you need their affection and attention.

• **Your parents may glorify your dead brother or sister.** Don't feel that this means that they really think he was "better" than you. Bereaved parents may temporarily forget that the child had faults like everyone else. You won't be able to live up to this glorified image, so don't even try. If you remember the person as he really was, you won't feel resentful.

• **The death of your sibling may make you fear that you'll be left alone.** It's not likely that both of your parents will die at the same time, but it could happen. When it seems to be the right time, ask your parent(s) who will care for you in such a situation.

• **Don't be afraid to talk about your sibling.** If your parents don't want to, find someone else to talk to. Often it's more painful when people don't mention your sibling than when they do.

• **Expect your parents to be overprotective.** They may worry that you will suffer the same fate as your sibling. This may seem irrational, but it's a fairly common grief reaction.

THE DEATH OF A PET

Some people may think it's silly, but the death of a pet can be a tremendous loss to anyone who considers a dog, cat, or other pet to be part of the family. Animals don't usually live as long as humans (although box turtles can live more than 120 years!), so the death of a pet can be your first experience with loss and grief. It can also prepare you for future losses and serve as a reminder that life is finite. Here are some things to keep in mind:

• **You should be told and understand why the pet died.** No one should try to protect you from the details of how your pet died, whether he died naturally, was hit by a car, or had to be put to sleep because he was ill.

• **You should trust your veterinarian to tell you when it is time for your pet to be put down**. Often, it is merciful to kill an animal to save him from suffering. Just as you wouldn't want a human being to suffer, you wouldn't want your pet to feel needless pain. Think about your pet's welfare as well as how you will feel when he's no longer with you.

• **If possible, the dead pet should be buried or cremated.** This provides an opportunity for you to say good-bye, and to say a few words about the love you felt for your pet. It's also an opportunity to talk about how bad you feel having lost a loyal friend.

• **You should be able to grieve for your pet.** Many people feel closer to their animals than they do to other humans. Just as a human death will make you sad or angry, the death of your pet will spark these feelings.

• **Your family shouldn't rush to get a new pet.** Pets are as irreplaceable as humans, and a new animal can't take the place of a beloved pet. The family should take time to get over the death of its pet. In time, however, if family members agree, getting a new pet can be a wonderful experience. New pets should be welcomed and loved as new members of the family. Just as we love many people, we can love many pets as well.

Many people feel closer to their animals than they do to other humans.

ACTIVITY: "THIS IS WHAT I WANT TO SAY"

It is hard to talk about death. Children need to feel comfortable expressing their feelings, and they need to know that whatever they're feeling—no matter how horrible—is okay. Here's what some teens said when asked what they wanted people to know about their grief. Write your thoughts about these statements beside them.

"I feel so bad. I feel like I should cry, but I can't. Why can't I cry?"

"I thought people went to hospitals to get better. Boy, was I wrong."

"The adults do nothing but cry. They won't even talk to me."

"The pain and hurt don't go away, they just get easier to deal with."

"I wish people would talk to me. It feels like _____'s death was my fault."

"I want someone to say, I don't know what to say, but I'll listen."

"I hate it when people tell me that everything will be okay."

"It's been three months, and no one talks about my dad anymore."

"I hate the feeling that I have to be strong for my younger siblings."

"I feel embarrassed by my mom's suicide."

ACTIVITY: UNFINISHED BUSINESS

When a loved one dies, there's usually some unfinished business, something we regret either saying or not saying, or doing or not doing. Complete these unfinished sentences to help you express your thoughts and feelings.

When you died, I felt _____ .

When I think about you, I feel _____ .

I wish we had _____ .

I wish I'd told you _____ .

I always wanted to ask you _____ .

I miss _____ .

I wish you had _____ .

I wish you'd told me _____ .

I'm mad because _____ .

I'm happy because _____

I'm angry because _____ .

If only _____ .

I'm glad that _____

STRESS MANAGEMENT

Stress Management

This chapter describes what stress is and how to manage it, and reviews the many causes, signs, and types of stress, including both chronic and "good" stress. Specific activities and coping skills are offered to help students determine if they are experiencing stress and ways to handle this feeling.

Time Allotment

Two 50-minute sessions integrated into a series of 50-minute class periods.

Goal

To help students learn coping skills to deal with stress.

Objectives

- A student will be able to verbalize the definition of stress.
- A student will be able to identify at least ten external factors that could lead to stressful feelings.
- A student will be able to verbalize two to three warning signs of physical, mental, and emotional stress.
- A student will be able to list four coping skills to deal with stress.

WHAT IS STRESS?

We hear so much about stress, and we all have our share of it. But what exactly is stress, and why is it so hard to manage?

Stress is the general feeling you have when too many things are going on in your life at once. These things don't have to be "bad" things—they can be things like planning a celebration, or anticipating a visit from an old friend, or even an upcoming life event, such as a graduation or holiday. Stress, of course, can be caused by negative events as well—getting a bad grade, worrying about college, dealing with an alcoholic parent, or just having a fight with someone. The list is almost endless.

When every one of your problems, everything you have to think about, every person you have to deal with, all become almost too much to bear . . . that's stress. As your life becomes more complicated, stress is the pressure you feel.

Never let anyone tell you that children don't feel stress. They do. Teens, in particular, may experience more stress than adults, because they are changing, sorting things out, and deciding who they are. If you think life is harder today than it was for your parents when they were your age, you're right. You may still be a kid, but you have lots of things to worry about—lots of things that can cause stress.

People have limits to the amount of pressure they can handle. When you're close to or at your limit, life can feel pretty bad. You can feel depressed, overwhelmed, and unable to cope. If you feel anxious or frightened, it's hard to sort out your troubles and to work on reducing stress. Your body reacts physically, too: your heart beats faster, your muscles tense up, and your blood pressure rises. You may feel nauseous, and you may break out in a sweat.

It's unfortunate that our society places so much emphasis on work and accomplishment. There's hardly any time left for relaxation and pleasure. Sometimes even the thought of doing "nothing"— reading, exercising, taking a bath, playing with a child—can cause a stress reaction, either because we feel guilty for taking the time, or upset that we don't have the time.

You have many years left in your life. Stress doesn't have to play a major role. You can learn to control it, live with it, and even benefit from it.

It's unfortunate that our society places so much emphasis on work and accomplishment.

Stress can be caused by many external factors, things beyond our control. Learning to deal with and reduce stress is key to learning to live a more healthy life.

Here's a list of events and situations that children and teens have said caused them stress. You'll see that some are serious, and others less important. That's part of the problem—stress can be caused by anything that makes you feel anxious and uncomfortable. You can add your stressors to the list.

- Drinking, drug use, violence, or sexual abuse at home
- Midterms or final exams
- The death or suicide of a friend or family member
- A change in schools
- Peer pressure or intimidation
- A move to another city or town
- Having an after-school job and not enough time to study
- Weapons at school
- Being smaller, taller, or otherwise different from most kids your age
- Coping with a mental or physical disability
- Dealing with a stepparent and/or stepfamily
- Being pressured to smoke or get high to fit in
- Discrimination or harassment because of your race, religion, gender, appearance, etc.
- Your parents' divorce or separation
- Being forced to do extracurricular activities
- Not fitting in with any social group
- Problems with friends
- High competition for grades
- The death or chronic illness of a loved one
- Being expected to get top grades all the time
- Not having anyone to talk to about what's bothering you
- Pressure to get into a good college and/or to pay for it
- Competition to make a sports team or other group
- Breaking up with a boyfriend or girlfriend
- Being jealous of a friend who has something you want
- Feeling competitive with a good friend
- Family financial problems

Stress can be caused by anything that makes you feel anxious and uncomfortable.

SIGNS OF STRESS

Everyone has stress. In fact, many stressful situations are unavoidable. Watching your parents fight, taking a really hard test, moving away from your friends, feeling powerless when a friend gets drunk or high, or worrying about college are part of life, whether you like it or not.

Too much stress can have a negative effect on your mind, body, and emotions. If you're able to deal with stress, you're probably more healthy than the person who is stressed-out all the time. When stress is overwhelming and lasts for a long time, it becomes distress.

Our bodies react to stress in certain ways. You don't have to be in actual danger to feel stress. Physical sensations can actually alert you to the fact that something's wrong, and they can make you stop and think "Why am I feeling this way?" Here are some typical signs of stress:

Too much stress can have a negative effect on your mind, body, and emotions.

Physical signs:

Headaches
Nervousness/anxiety
Cool hands and feet
Feeling warm in the face
Dry mouth
Rashes
Stomachaches

Fast heartbeat
Perspiration/clammy hands
Crying for no apparent reason
Wanting to eat all the time
Not wanting to eat at all
Sleeping a lot
Not sleeping at all

Mental signs:

Lack of concentration
Forgetfulness
Drop in school performance

Inability to study
Carelessness
Withdrawal from friends

Emotional signs:

Boredom
Outbursts of anger
Nightmares

Sadness/depression
Feeling scared
Picking fights

CHRONIC STRESS

Have you heard the expression "fight or flight?" The fight-or-flight response happens when we are hit with a stressful situation. We must choose instantly whether to stand our ground and combat the source of stress or to run for safety. How you choose to handle stress can determine how well you feel physically and emotionally.

Chronic, or long-term, stress is usually what people are talking about when they say they're "stressed out." Some of the stressors are totally out of your control, such as divorce or a really hard class. Having a very busy unchangeable schedule can also cause chronic stress. The problem with this kind of stress is that it can sneak up on you.

Consider these facts:

• We all have stressors that we can't do anything about, such as school rules, homework, and feeling unsafe.

• We have so much to do that we can't stop and rest, and this causes stress.

• We're products of our "driven" culture: driven to be productive, driven to succeed, driven to win.

• Most people don't know how to relax, and many feel guilty when they do.

• Most people have a problem saying no when someone asks them to do something, even if they are already overloaded.

• We're so busy that we skip meals, don't get enough sleep, and generally let our bodies run down.

When you're stressed out, you have little energy, and it becomes more and more difficult to sort things out. Your body knows when it's time to stop, and it tells you so in many ways, but at this point your mind is usually not ready to admit defeat. It's amazing how many things you can say to yourself to keep going. But sooner or later, your mind and body are going to need attention, in one way or another.

If you feel that you are reaching your limit, and that one more thing will drive you over the edge, it's time to begin to learn to deal with stress.

GOOD STRESS

This may be hard to believe, but we all need some stress in our lives. Stress prepares us to deal with life. Too little stress can be boring, and too much stress can be devastating. But some stress is good, even necessary.

Here's an example of good stress. Robin's parents tell her that they are going to be moving to another city and that they understand how upsetting this is for her. They don't realize Robin is secretly excited about the prospect of making new friends and starting fresh. Her old friends have been using drugs, and she's been on the outs with them. However, she feels nervous too. As she looks forward, she feels stress, but mostly good stress. Of course, if she weren't unhappy with her current situation, she'd probably feel scared and sad to move, causing some bad stress.

Here's another example. Clay's been thinking about finals week for about a month now. He's made a plan to go over his notes for one subject each week until the finals begin. After each test during finals week, he plans to come home and study intensely for the next day's test. He thinks this is a good plan, but he still feels nervous and edgy. This is a natural reaction—who wouldn't be nervous about finals? But he's got the situation under control, and he knows that if he follows this plan, he's got a good chance of doing well. He's feeling necessary stress, but it's good stress.

Good stress motivates you, helps you achieve, and enables you to solve problems. The more good stress you have, the easier it is to deal with what life brings your way.

It's important to keep things in perspective. You shouldn't worry about unforeseen events in the future. You cannot control them and needless worrying causes stress. If you can step back from a situation, plan for it, and put it in perspective, you'll be able to minimize your stress, learn from it, and be better prepared for the next stressor. This will give you a sense of power that in turn will help to relieve stress.

Good stress motivates you, helps you achieve, and enables you to solve problems.

BEWARE THE PERFECTION SYNDROME

You need to be realistic about your fears and assess the consequences if you perform less than perfectly.

Many children are under constant stress because they are expected to perform in a certain manner. This pressure comes initially from adults including parents and teachers, but ultimately it becomes part of the child's psyche, and the pressure to be perfect becomes too much to bear.

It's important to keep things in perspective, to realize that you cannot control everything, even your actions and thoughts.

Sometimes anticipation is actually worse than the dreaded event itself. Have you ever been nervous before a test only to find out that it wasn't nearly as hard as you expected? What's the worst that could happen if you didn't do well? You need to be realistic about your fears and assess the consequences if you perform less than perfectly. Probably you are overestimating the negative. This is the kind of advice you would give a friend. It's also the advice you should give yourself.

If you've been programmed to do your best for other people, perhaps it's time to look at what you want for yourself and your future. Maybe your family has always included doctors or star football players. If you're following in the family footsteps and you're content to fit the mold, that's fine. But if you're not really sure whether the mold is right for you, it's time to decide what you want to do instead.

And remember: If you decide to pursue other interests and these don't quite measure up, that's okay too. The idea is to keep your options open, try new things, and widen your horizons. This is the only way you'll really know who you are and what you want to do.

IF YOU FEEL STRESSED . . .

. . . and you have little or no time to slow down, taking just a few minutes to breathe deeply can help. Here are three stress-relieving exercises that will take little or no time:

If you feel stressed and have only 30 seconds:
- Close your eyes.
- Inhale deeply through your nose and hold it for a few seconds.
- Exhale slowly through your mouth. Repeat these steps a few times.
- Inhale as much air as you can through your mouth, then let it out slowly, as if you were sighing. Do this a few times.

If you feel stressed and have only a minute:
- Close your eyes.
- Picture yourself in a peaceful place where you have felt totally relaxed in the past: for example, a beach, floating on a raft, lying in a field.
- Inhale deeply through your nose, and focus on the picture in your mind.
- Exhale very slowly through your mouth. Keep imagining the picture.
- After a minute, open your eyes.
- Use your lips to make sounds as you breathe. Don't use your voice.
- Do this several times, breathing deeply and concentrating on the sounds.

If you feel stressed and have 5 or 10 minutes:
- Lie on your bed or sit in a chair.
- Start by focusing on your feet, and tighten the muscles in them while you count to five.
- Relax these muscles and move up to the next part of your body. Do this until you get to your face.
- Breathe slowly and deeply as you contract each part of your body.
- When you're finished, lie or sit still for a few minutes and concentrate on your breathing.
- Take a bath or shower.
- Listen to a relaxing CD.

There are many ways of handling stress. The important thing is to be aware that you're experiencing it before it invades your life completely.

Here are some ways to cope:

- **Practice relaxation methods.** Do deep breathing exercises, or imagine yourself in a peaceful place.

- **Think positive thoughts.** Think about something good that happened, or someone you like and why that person likes you.

- **Find time to relax and cool down.** Take a bath, take a walk, or read a magazine—anything that will calm you.

- **Visualize what you want to happen.** Practice saying "no" and using "I" messages. Convince yourself that you don't have to be perfect.

- **Talk about it.** Find a friend, teacher, counselor, or family member who will listen to and really hear you.

- **Don't dwell on weaknesses.** Think about your strengths and accomplishments, and feel proud of them.

- **Exercise daily.** Running, walking, working out—any form of exercise— makes you feel better and more ready for stressors.

- **Punch a pillow, kick a can, or scream.** Get your stress and tension out in a safe manner and place.

- **Eat well.** Nutritious snacks and meals make all the difference in the way you feel.

- **Don't procrastinate.** If you're worried about a test, study for it—now. Take care of annoying business sooner rather than later.

- **Set realistic goals.** Do one task at a time; don't start a new one until you've finished the last one.

- **Don't worry about things that may or may not happen.** Worrying won't help—it'll just make you more anxious.

- **Make time for fun.** Get involved in things you like to do, and do things for others, too.

Take a bath, take a walk, or read a magazine — anything that will calm you.

Take care of annoying business sooner rather than later.

ACTIVITY: STRESS SYMPTOMS AND RELIEVERS

I know I'm stressed out when I:

- [ ] Can't sleep
- [ ] Sleep too much
- [ ] Feel anxious and nervous
- [ ] Eat too much or not enough
- [ ] Resort to smoking
- [ ] Use alcohol and/or drugs
- [ ] Cry over little things
- [ ] Yell at everyone a lot
- [ ] Have an acne flair-up
- [ ] Become overly sensitive
- [ ] Feel fidgety all the time
- [ ] Can't get out of bed
- [ ] Feel dizzy and/or "fuzzy"

When I'm experiencing these symptoms, I:

- [ ] Go for a walk or run
- [ ] Read a good book (not a school book)
- [ ] Exercise for at least 30 minutes
- [ ] Write a letter or email to a friend
- [ ] Write in my journal (or start a journal)
- [ ] Listen to soothing music
- [ ] Take deep breaths and relax for a while
- [ ] Bake a cake or cookies
- [ ] Go shopping for something I really want
- [ ] Talk to a friend/family member/counselor/teacher/_____
- [ ] Confront the situation and say "no"
- [ ] Use assertiveness techniques
- [ ] Talk to the person I'm angry with and use "I" messages
- [ ] Eliminate one of my responsibilities
- [ ] Do something I really like to do

ACTIVITY: DON'T SWEAT THE STRESSORS

Stressors do not have to be major life events. Everyday things can stress you: getting a bad grade, having a fight with your brother, not getting the birthday present you wanted. Anything that makes you feel sad, angry, nervous, or uncomfortable can cause stress. Read the first example on this page and fill in the blanks for the rest of it.

The stressor was: *I forgot to clean my room this morning and my parents aren't giving me my allowance this week.*

My reaction was: *Anger, but when I think about it, I was more mad at myself, because my parents warned me that this would happen.*

I'm not going to sweat it, because: *I guess I deserved what I got. I just won't be able to buy anything this week. I know they want me to be more responsible, so I guess I'll try.*

The stressor was: _____

_____.

My reaction was: _____

_____.

I'm not going to sweat it, because: _____

_____.

The stressor was: _____

_____.

My reaction was: _____

_____.

I'm not going to sweat it, because: _____

_____.

SOURCES

Chapter 1: Improving Motivation

- Benson, P., Galbraith, J., & Espeland, P. 1998. *What Teens Need to Succeed.* Minneapolis: Free Spirit.
- Hey Teach! How to Get Along with Your Teachers. http://www.kidshealth.org
- Lewis, B. 1998. *What Do You Stand For? A Kid's Guide to Building Character.* Minneapolis: Free Spirit.
- Mandel, H., & Marcus, S. 1995. *Could Do Better: Why Children Underachieve and What to Do About It.* New York: John Wiley.
- Schoel, J., Prouty, D., & Radcliffe, P. 1988. *Islands of Healing.* Hamilton, MA: Project Adventure.
- Schunk, D., & Zimmerman, B., Eds. 1994. *Self-Regulation of Learning and Performance.* Hillsdale, NJ: Lawrence Erlbaum.
- Study Skills. http://www.homeworkcentral.com

Chapter 2: Successful Relationships

- Benson, P., Galbraith, J., & Espeland, P. 1998. *What Teens Need to Succeed.* Minneapolis: Free Spirit.
- Fact sheet. Gerken, K. 1992. "Children and peer relations." In *Helping Children Grow Up in the 90s.* Silver Spring, MD: National Association of Social Workers.
- Hipp, E. 1995. *Fighting Invisible Tigers: A Stress Management Guide for Teens.* Minneapolis: Free Spirit.
- Packer, A. 1992. *Bringing Up Parents: The Teenager's Handbook.* Minneapolis: Free Spirit.

Chapter 3: Increasing Self-Esteem

- Benson, P., Galbraith, J., & Espeland, P. 1998. *What Teens Need to Succeed.* Minneapolis: Free Spirit.
- Do You Have Low Esteem? http://www.srg.co.uk/howareyou.html
- Fact sheet. 1992. "Children and self-esteem." In *Helping Children Grow Up in the 90s.* Silver Spring, MD: National Association of Social Workers.
- Johnson, D., & Johnson, R. 1991. *Teaching Students to Be Peacemakers.* Edina, MN: Interaction Book Co.
- McCoy, N., & Wibblesman, C. 1996. *Life Happens.* New York: Perigee.
- Recognizing My Positive Qualities/Positive Thinking vs. Mental Misery: Empower Yourself. http://www.uiuc.edu
- Taylor-Gerdes, E. 1994. *Straight Up!* Chicago: Lindsey Publishing.

SOURCES

Chapter 4: Dealing with Anger

- Bochnowicz, J. 1999. Anger as a Secondary Emotion. Bucks County, PA: Bucks County Peace Center.
- Johnson, D., & Johnson, R. 1991. *Teaching Students to Be Peacemakers*.
  Edina, MN: Interaction Book Co.
- Reminders/Trigger Thoughts. http://scribers.midwest.net

Chapter 5: Conflict Resolution

- Benson, P., Galbraith, J., & Espeland, P. 1998. *What Teens Need to Succeed*.
  Minneapolis: Free Spirit.
- Bolton, R. 1979. *People Skills: How to Assert Yourself, Listen to Others, and Resolve Conflicts*.
  New York: Simon & Schuster.
- Deutsch, M. 1991. "Educating for a Peaceful World." Presented to the Division of Peace Psychology,
  American Psychological Association, July, 1991.
- Drew, N. 1987. *Learning the Skills of Peacemaking*. Rolling Hills Estates, CA: Jalmar Press.
- Johnson, D., & Johnson, R. 1991. *Teaching Students to Be Peacemakers*.
  Edina, MN: Interaction Book Co.
- Kreidler, W. 1984. *Creative Conflict Resolution*. Glenview, IL: Scott, Foresman and Co.
- Schulman, M., & Mekler, E. 1994. *Bringing Up a Moral Child*. New York: Doubleday.
- Shore, H. 1995. *Let's Work It Out! A Conflict Resolution Toolkit*.
  Plainview, NY: Bureau for At-Risk Youth.

Chapter 6: Violence Awareness

- Checklist of Characteristics of Youth Who Have Caused School-Associated Violent Deaths.
  http://www.nssc1.org
- Early Warning, Timely Response: A Guide to Safe Schools. http://www.air-dc.org
- Gorin, S. 1999. National Association of Pupil Services Administration (NAPSA).
  The Topic Was Violence in Schools. Vol. XXXIV, No. 3.
- Jacobs, T. 1997. *What Are My Rights? 95 Questions and Answers About Teens and the Law*.
  Minneapolis: Free Spirit.
- McCoy, N., & Wibblesman, C. 1996. *Life Happens*. New York: Perigee.
- Schaefer, C., & DiGeronimo, T. 1999. *How to Talk to Teens About Really Important Things*.
  San Francisco: Jossey-Bass.
- Schwarz, T. 1999. *Kids and Guns*. New York: Franklin Watts.
- Scott, S. 1997. *How to Say No and Keep Your Friends*.
  Amherst, MA: Human Resource Development Press.
- Statman, P. 1995. *On the Safe Side: Teach Your Child to Be Safe, Strong, and Street-Smart*.
  New York: HarperPerennial.
- Teenagers and Risks. http://www.cnn.com/HEALTH/mayo
- Youth Violence. http://www.pcvp.org
- Youth Violence in the United States Fact Sheet. http://www.cdc.gov

SOURCES

Chapter 7: Coping with Depression

- Cobain, B. 1998. *When Nothing Matters Anymore*. Minneapolis: Free Spirit.
- Crist, J. 1996. *ADHD: A Teenager's Guide*. Plainview, NY: Childswork/Childsplay.
- Depression.com. http://www.depression.com
- Dubuque, S. & Dubuque, N. 1996. *Kid Power Tactics for Dealing with Depression*. Plainview, NY: Childswork/Childsplay.
- National Network for Childcare. http://www.nncc.org
- Wing of Madness: A Depression Guide. http://www.wingofmadness.com

Chapter 8: Resolving Family Issues

- Forward, S. 1989. *Toxic Parents*. New York: Bantam.
- Lee, V. 1990. *Dysfunctional Families*. Vero Beach, FL: Rourke Corp.
- Paris, T., & Paris, E. 1992. *I'll Never Do to My Kids What My Parents Did to Me!* New York: Warner.
- Strommen, M., & Strommen, A. 1985. *Five Cries of Parents*. New York: HarperCollins.

Chapter 9: The Effects of Divorce

- Berry, J. 1990. *Good Answers to Tough Questions About Divorce*. Chicago: Children's Press.
- Divorce Central. http://www.divorcecentral.com
- Field, M. 1992. *All About Divorce*. King of Prussia, PA: Center for Applied Psychology.
- Flood, N., & Nichols, M. 1998. *The Counseling Handbook*. Secaucus, NJ: Childswork/Childsplay.
- Mental Health Net. http://mentalhelp.net
- Nickman, S. (1986) *When Mom and Dad Divorce*. New York: Julian Messner.
- Teyber, E. 1992. *Helping Children Cope with Divorce*. New York: Lexington Books.
- Your Parents' Divorce. http://www.odos.uiuc.edu/Counseling_Center/divorce.htm

Chapter 10: Are You Assertive?

- Are You Assertive? http://www.queendom.com/assert.html
- Assertiveness Now! http://mentalhelp.net/articles/grohol/assert.htm
- Basic Strategies for Behaving More Assertively. http://www.unc.edu/depts/unc_caps/Assert.html
- Benson, P., Galbraith, J., & Espeland, P. 1998. *What Teens Need to Succeed*. Minneapolis: Free Spirit.
- Folkers, G., & Engelmann, J. 1997, *Taking Charge of My Mind and Body*. Minneapolis: Free Spirit.
- Hipp, E. 1995. *Fighting Invisible Tigers: A Stress Management Guide for Teens*. Minneapolis: Free Spirit.
- How Assertive Are You? http://www.srg.co.uk/areyouassert.html
- Madaras, L., & Madaras, A. 1993. *Growing Up Guide for Girls*. New York: Newmarket Press.
- Prochaska, J., Norcross, J., & DiClemente, C. 1994. *Changing for Good*. New York: Avon.

SOURCES

Chapter 11: Understanding Eating Disorders

- The Eating Disorders Site. http://www.somethingfishy.org
- Foreyt, J., & McGavin, J. 1989. "Anorexia Nervosa and Bulimia Nervosa."
  In E. Mash & R. Barkley (Eds.) *Treatment of Childhood Disorders*. New York: Guilford.
- Gracie Square Hospital. Eating Disorders Program Fact Sheet. New York: Author.
- Harvard Eating Disorders Center. http://www.hedc.org
- Irilli, J., & Carty, C. 1992. "Children and Anorexia and Bulimia."
  In *Helping Children Grow Up in the 90s*. Silver Spring, MD: National Association of Social Workers.
- Parenting Q&A. http://www.parenting-qa.com
- Slap-Shelton, L. 1996. "Childhood and Adolescent Eating Disorders." In H. Shore (Ed.)
  Child Therapy Today, Vol. II. King of Prussia, PA: Center for Applied Psychology.

Chapter 12: Overcoming Substance Abuse

- The Art of Healing. http://www.artdsm.com
- Dimoff, T., & Carper, S. 1992. *How to Tell If Your Kids are Using Drugs*. New York: Facts on File.
- Folkers, G., & Engelmann, J. 1997. *Taking Charge of My Mind and Body*. Minneapolis: Free Spirit.
- Malekoff, A. 1997. *Group Work with Adolescents*. New York: Guilford.
- Randolph, M., Forman, S., & Jackson, K. 1992. "Children and Drug Abuse."
  In *Helping Children Grow Up in the 90s*. Silver Spring, MD: National Association of Social Workers.
- Scott, S. 1997. *How to Say No and Keep Your Friends*.
  Amherst, MA: Human Resource Development Press.
- Shore, H. 1998. "Nicotine Addiction in Young People."
  In H. Shore (Ed.) *Child Therapy Today, Vol. IV*. Plainview, NY: Childswork/Childsplay.
- Teens: Alcohol and Other Drugs. http://www.aacap.org/factsfam/teendrug.htm
- What to Do If You or a Friend is Dealing with a Drug or Alcohol Addiction.
  http://kidshealth.org/teen

Chapter 13: Suicide Assessment and Intervention

- Frankel, B., & Kranz, R. 1994. *Straight Talk About Teenage Suicide*. New York: Facts on File.
- MacLean, G. 1990. *Suicide in Children and Adolescents*. Lewiston, NY: Hogrefe & Huber.
- Shore, H. 1998. "Suicide in Children and Adolescents."
  In H. Shore (Ed.) *The Child Therapy News, Vol. VI, No. 1*. Plainview, NY: Childswork/Childsplay.
- Slaby, A., & Garfinkel, L. 1994. *No One Saw My Pain: Why Teens Kills Themselves*. New York: Norton.
- Suicide: Read This First/ Handling a Call from a Suicidal Person/What Can I Do to Help Someone
  Who May Be Suicidal? http://www.metanoia.org/suicide/
- Teen Suicide. http://mentalhelp.net/factsfam/suicide.htm

SOURCES

Chapter 14: Grief and Loss

- Donnelly, K. 1988. *Recovering from the Loss of a Sibling*, New York: Dodd, Mead & Co.
- Fitzgerald, H. 1992. *The Grieving Child*. New York: Fireside.
- Goldman, L. 1996. *Breaking the Silence*. Philadelphia: Accelerated Development.
- Grollman, E. (Ed.) 1995. *Bereaved Children and Teens*. Boston: Beacon Press.
- Grollman, E. 1993. *Straight Talk About Death for Teenagers*. Boston: Beacon Press.
- Heath, C. 1992. *Children and reactions to death*. NASP book.
- Helping Teenagers Cope with Grief. http://hpmc.ca/topic-p3.htm
- Lightner, C., & Hathaway, N. 1990. *Giving Sorrow Words*. New York: Warner Books.
- Schaefer, D., & Lyons, C. 1986. *How Do We Tell the Children?* New York: Newmarket Press.
- Shore, H. 1996. "Helping Children Cope with Death." In H. Shore (Ed.) *Child Therapy Today, Vol. II.* Plainview, NY: Childswork/Childsplay.
- Stages Children Go Through When They Are Grieving/Surviving the Holidays. http://www.death-dying.com
- TAG: Teen Age Grief. http://www.smartlink.net
- What Is Complicated Grief? http://users.erols.com/lgold/info.htm

Chapter 15: Stress Management

- Don't Stress Out! http://www.girlzone.com/html_98-01/insideout.html
- Folkers, G., & Engelmann, J. 1997. *Taking Charge of My Mind and Body*. Minneapolis: Free Spirit.
- Helping Your Teenager with Stress. http://www.ces.ncsu.edu
- Hipp, E. 1995. *Fighting Invisible Tigers: A Stress Management Guide for Teens*. Minneapolis: Free Spirit.
- McCoy, N., & Wibblesman, C. 1996. *Life Happens*. New York: Perigee.
- Spotlight on Stress. http://macad.org/referral/